TUNNEL VIS

TUNNEL VISION

Ken Cordner

Ian Allan

PUBLISHING

First Published in 2008

ISBN 978 0 7110 3342 9

© Ken Cordner 2008

Published by Ian Allan Publishing

an imprint of Ian Allan Publishing Ltd, Hersham, Surrey KT12 4RG
Printed in England by Ian Allan Printing

Code: 0811/B3

Visit the Ian Allan Publishing website at www.ianallanpublishing.co.uk

Previous page:
*Passengers leave (and some stop to photograph) a Eurostar train that has arrived in
platform 10 at St Pancras on the first day of services there, 14 November 2007.* LCR/TROIKA

Contents

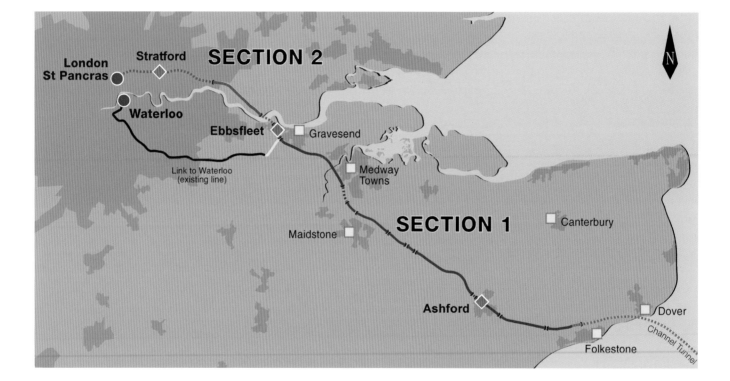

An overview map of the Channel Tunnel Rail Link.

Introduction

THE CHANNEL TUNNEL RAIL LINK – 'High Speed 1', as it was dubbed in 2006 – is the first major new railway in Great Britain for more than 100 years, and the country's first high-speed line.

Plans for a Channel Tunnel Rail Link (CTRL) have a long history, full of political, commercial, planning and environmental considerations. When a Channel Tunnel eventually began to be built in the late 1980s, pressure grew – not least from Channel Tunnel concessionaire Eurotunnel – to provide a new railway between London and the Tunnel terminal near Folkestone, which would service the tunnel's capacity for international rail traffic and provide rapid overall journey times. Though early studies were allowed to take only limited account of wider benefits, in later work train services using the CTRL for faster journeys between Kent and London, and regeneration of surrounding areas, were to become added justifications for the new railway.

Initial plans, largely based on the widening of existing rail routes, gave way to a solution staying close to existing motorways and railways where possible, still penetrating London by tunnelling. For many people living close to the proposed routes, the best place for a new railway was naturally somewhere else or, failing that, in a tunnel or deep trench, out of sight or hearing. In east London, however, Newham Council actively campaigned to have the Channel Tunnel Rail Link come its way, complete with a local station, because of the potential assistance this could give to economic regeneration.

Labour-led Newham's view fitted neatly with the plans for regeneration in a Thames-side corridor east of London, promoted by Michael Heseltine, who headed the Department of the Environment in John Major's Conservative Government from late 1990. The easterly approach to London finally chosen for the CTRL also relieved pressure (including that on Conservative MPs) against routes via south London and west Kent.

Regeneration benefits from international and domestic train services for Kent were also a consideration. At Ashford, local pressure brought the Channel Tunnel Rail Link through the urban centre rather than on a by-pass route.

By the time the new line opened, the commercial policies of Eurostar had resulted in a reduced service for Ashford, and had consigned to disuse, for now, the links constructed near the CTRL's new London terminal to give direct access to the West and East Coast Main Lines, as well as the link from the CTRL to London Waterloo. But there is pressure for a 'High Speed 2', which could spring from the junctions with HS1 near St Pancras and provide railway speed and capacity improvements for a major artery to the north of London.

This book starts with a chronology of the plans for a Channel Tunnel Rail Link and its eventual realisation. It also describes the main features of the CTRL as completed in 2007, and provides a year-by-year account of its construction.

Better than thousands of words are the superb mapping kindly provided by Trackmaps and the photographs provided by courtesy of London & Continental Railways and individual photographers.

Many thanks are also due to all the staff of London & Continental Railways and its associated companies who have helped with interviews and background information throughout the nine years of the Channel Tunnel Rail Link's construction.

1966

British and French Prime Ministers, Wilson and Pompidou, announce that Channel Tunnel is to be built.

1971

Anglo-French agreement reached with two consortia on studies for Channel Tunnel. British Rail (BR) and French Railways (SNCF) work on scheme to link Channel Tunnel to Paris and London. Existing UK routes, with improvements, are thought to have adequate capacity. BR believes new London terminal is needed at Kensington Olympia or Clapham Junction, with interchange near Ashford, Kent, as continental-gauge trains would not be able to run any further.

1973

Anglo-French agreement reached on detailed studies for Channel Tunnel. British Government decides new rail link to London will be needed.

1974

BR publishes proposals on route to be used via Ashford, Tonbridge and Croydon – with possible by-passes, additional tracks or tunnels at Ashford, Tonbridge and at London end of route.

1975

Channel Tunnel and £373 million rail link project abandoned by UK Government on grounds of cost.
BR and SNCF put forward series of Channel Tunnel proposals over following decade.

1986

Channel Tunnel concession awarded by UK and French Governments.

1987

Channel Tunnel Act passed. Includes provision of additional capacity on existing rail network but, with domestic rail traffic falling, does not assume new rail link is needed and specifically rules out Government support for construction.
Improvements to existing routes begin, with development of Waterloo International station and Wembley freight centre. Work completed in 1993 at cost of £1.7 billion.

Opposite:

A spectacular light show during the Royal opening on 6 November 2007. LCR/Eddie Macdonald

Department of Transport's Kent Impact Study suggests that while capacity of existing network between London and Channel Tunnel would be sufficient to handle international traffic until end of century, new high-speed line would then be required.

1988

BR studies of capacity and future demand suggest additional facilities will be required, and four route options for new rail link are published, provoking hostile public reaction in areas affected.

1989

January: King's Cross announced as location for second London terminal, an eight-platform below-ground station for UK and international services, including improved cross-London 'Thameslink 2000' route.

March: Preferred route for Channel Tunnel rail link is announced after confidential discussions with local authorities; it runs in tunnel from King's Cross, surfacing to form junction with existing route to/from Waterloo at Peckham Rye, then in tunnel to near Swanley, with further 4-mile tunnel under North Downs, then largely following M20 motorway and passing through centre of Ashford.

Twenty-three miles of 68-mile route would be in tunnel; cost is put at £1.7 billion compared with £1.2 billion for broadly similar Route 2 of 1988. One-third of cost is for environmental protection.

Maximum 225km/h (140mph) speed is proposed, to limit environmental impacts, and 240-metre voluntary purchase zone is established for residential property.

Predictions are of 17 to 21 million passenger journeys per year in 2003, and 7 to 10 million tonnes of freight.

September: After stormy consultation period and assessment of rival route options (including one in tunnel all the way from Channel Tunnel to Essex), refined route is published.

October: Eurorail joint venture of Trafalgar House and BICC is selected to develop Channel Tunnel Rail Link, but proposed submission of Parliamentary Bill is delayed for a year when it finds commercial funding is not possible. Alternatives to high-cost tunnel into London are sought, with possible addition of a west Kent parkway station as possible revenue generator.

1990

June: Transport Secretary in Conservative Government, Cecil Parkinson, announces that joint venture's proposals cannot be accepted as they require Government support. He asks for further work on Medway-London route options, study of routes proposed by other parties, and improvement of benefits to international and domestic passengers, with freight strategies taken into account. Joint venture is dissolved, but Mid Kent to Channel Tunnel route is safeguarded and consultation continues on refinement.

BR project group begins study of three alternative proposed routes to Stratford, east London, terminal via Thames crossing at either Dartford (Arup proposal) or Tilbury (Eurorail), or in tunnel from Hither Green (London Borough of Newham proposal). With extensions to King's Cross, they are assessed against version of BR route with London tunnel starting at Hither Green. BR sets up separate project team to develop King's Cross low-level station.

November: John Major becomes Prime Minister in place of Margaret Thatcher, and Michael Heseltine heads Department of the Environment; impetus is given to work on what is later dubbed Thames Gateway – a Thames-side regeneration zone running eastwards from London.

1991

May: Report to Government recommends southerly rail link approach to Waterloo and King's Cross, but ranks the Arup route best of easterly approach options.

October: Transport Secretary Malcolm Rifkind asks for refinement of Arup route proposal, expecting it ultimately to be taken forward by private sector. He says route maximises development potential in east London/lower Thames, removes property blight in south London and west Kent, and minimises impact on environment and property. Route is estimated to cost £3.9 to £4.5 billion. BR estimates it has spent £140 million on work on southern route and property purchase.

1992

BR agency company Union Railways set up to develop Channel Tunnel Rail Link, working with private sector groups Arup, Eurolink (Trafalgar House/Balfour Beatty), Halcrow, Gibb, Mott MacDonald, and Scott Wilson Kirkpatrick, plus environmental consultancies.

1993

Report to Government by Union Railways leaves final decisions to Government: it presents Reference Case maximising financial performance while meeting environmental standards generally applied to major infrastructure projects. Other options for Government consideration are ranked by cost-benefit analysis of economic benefits of domestic services, and possible enhanced environmental mitigation.

March: Government chooses to take Reference Case forward to consultation, but with more expensive option of following A2/M2 corridor (between km39 and 62 of final route). This crosses Medway on high-level viaduct, rather than low-level one upstream at Halling.

Route for consultation is announced after route options are compared on engineering, environmental, planning and business grounds, in a 'sifting' process carried out with confidential involvement of most local authorities, and of Government departments. Choice is still to be made between alternative terminals at King's Cross low level or St Pancras (latter predicted to cost less).

1994

January: Government chooses St Pancras as London terminal, and confirms more lengthy M2 corridor route at Medway crossing, with cut-and-cover tunnels further east for environmental mitigation at Hollingbourne and Sandway.

Revised route at Ashford (through town centre rather than by-passing it, politically preferred despite need for greater demolition) and revised route further from housing at Pepper Hill near Gravesend are left open: after rapid assessment process, these revisions are agreed by April.

Government acquires Union Railways and Eurostar from British Rail as agency companies, and in March launches competition to find private-sector consortium to take Channel Tunnel Rail Link (CTRL) forward.

May: Channel Tunnel (and high-speed link in France) officially opened.

November: Channel Tunnel Rail Link bill – hybrid (Government-supported) bill – submitted to Parliament, accompanied by one of the most comprehensive Environmental Statements ever produced in UK.

1995

After considering objections, main conclusions of longest-running House of Commons Select Committee to consider hybrid or private bill are:
* ruling against combined structure for CTRL and second M2 motorway crossing of Medway
* inclusion of freight connections at Dollands Moor (giving direct access to new railway for largest international railfreight vehicles) and at Dagenham (leading to Ripple Lane freight yard and existing network), with two sets of passing loops on CTRL
* rejection of long North Downs tunnel, but adoption of deeper cutting in Boxley valley
* adoption of international loading gauge through Ashford station
* confirmation of Ebbsfleet station
* movement of route at Purfleet and Rainham in Essex to reduce impact
* extension of London tunnel to Dagenham instead of using existing Barking-Dagenham surface railway corridor
* adoption of long below-ground box to keep open option of station construction at Stratford.

1996

29 February: Chosen private-sector consortium, London & Continental Railways (LCR), and Government sign development agreement for CTRL project. LCR members are Arup, Bechtel, Halcrow, London Electricity, National Express, Systra, Virgin, and SG Warburg. In complex package, subsidy totalling about £1.4 billion is agreed, with Eurostar debt of about £1.3 billion written off. LCR gains St Pancras station, and railway land at King's Cross and Stratford, with development profits to be split with Government. Support is also included for services from Kent via CTRL, and there is also additional Government money for cross-London 'Thameslink 2000' railway development scheme, expected to be started soon by Railtrack, which will cover some of works to be carried out at St Pancras. CTRL is planned to open in 2003.

LCR plans to build Stratford international and domestic station, with direct link from CTRL at St Pancras leading to West Coast Main Line (via North London Line). These additions later authorised via Transport & Works Act order.

House of Lords Select Committee, considering CTRL bill after hearing objections:
* concludes that scheme is overall as sensitive to landscape as can reasonably be expected
* rejects longer tunnel at North Downs, but selects lowered alignment in Boxley valley
* adopts alignment keeping under North London Line for St Pancras approaches
* decides to limit landtake by using steep retaining walls at Horish and Honeyhills woodlands in Detling, north of Maidstone
* refers issue of residential property blight to interdepartmental Government working group.

18 December: CTRL bill is enacted, just over two years after submission.

Although Act gives powers to build and operate new railway, detailed planning consent has to be sought from local authorities, who can influence and control detailed design and mitigation.

1997

Consortium to design and manage construction of CTRL is set up. Later known as Rail Link Engineering, it is made up of LCR's engineering shareholders: Bechtel, Ove Arup, Halcrow, and Systra.

April: First tenders issued for construction.

1998

January: LCR announces it cannot raise finance for CTRL as Eurostar profits cannot support flotation. (LCR had envisaged raising about £800 million through stock exchange flotation, with loans to cover peak financial debt requirement estimated at £3.2 billion.)

Government rejects LCR proposals for additional support, but allows alternative package to be developed.

June: John Prescott, Deputy Prime Minister in Labour Government elected in 1997, announces that CTRL will be built in two sections to allow participation of national rail network's infrastructure company, Railtrack, which is intended to manage construction, then acquire whole CTRL.

Railtrack will buy Section One (from Channel Tunnel to north Kent) and take on financial risk, with option to buy Section Two (north Kent to London). Pain-gain sharing mechanisms relating to Eurostar cashflow and access charge payments involve Railtrack and new operating consortium for Eurostar. Government grant is rescheduled but not increased (approximately £3.5 billion at 1997 prices, including more than £1 billion in payments for capacity for domestic services over 17 years) and Government agrees to guarantee £3.75 billion of debt, as well as Eurostar access charge payments. Government takes stakeholder share in LCR, entitling it to share of company's cash flow after 2020 and share of proceeds of any future sale of LCR or its assets. CTRL and Eurostar concession is reduced from 999 to 90 years.

Tendering for CTRL construction restarts; first civil contracts awarded in September.

15 October: John Prescott officially marks start of construction at traditional ground-breaking ceremony where CTRL's Medway crossing will be built near Cuxton in Kent.

2000

Track, signalling, and power contracts let in early 2000, with tenders invited in June for Section Two civils work.

2001

April: After Railtrack's financial difficulties following Hatfield accident in 2000, LCR takes on responsibility for CTRL Section Two, backed by cost-overrun protection from Bechtel – partly on its own account, partly through insurance. Railtrack is still to operate and maintain whole CTRL. Construction cost of Section Two is put at £1.9 billion, rising to £3.3 billion including financing and property.

2 July: Section Two major construction work starts. On 30 July North Downs tunnel in Section One is completed.

August: Two sides of Medway Viaduct are joined.

On 15 October 1998 the Deputy Prime Minister, John Prescott, breaks the first ground for the Channel Tunnel Rail Link, on the west bank of the Medway in Kent.
BRIAN MORRISON

Breakthrough of Britain's first high-speed railway tunnel under the North Downs on 8 June 2000: Deputy Prime Minister John Prescott points to where a 'road header' (excavator with a rotating grinder on a movable arm) is emerging behind him. LCR/QA Photos

The Eurostar train that set a UK speed record of 334.7km/h (208mph) on the CTRL crosses the Medway, eastbound, during the high-speed exploits on 30 July 2003. LCR

2002

29 August: First tunnel-boring machine for London tunnels is launched westwards from Stratford.

October: As result of Railtrack being placed in administration in October 2001, CTRL returns to unified management and ownership. LCR completes acquisition of Railtrack UK (holding company for CTRL interests) for £375 million, and LCR sells Railtrack's successor Network Rail right to operate CTRL and St Pancras station for £80 million. To replace funding from Railtrack's proposed purchase of CTRL Section One, LCR uses bonds and bank loans securitised on Eurostar access charges (guaranteed by Government in 1998) and domestic services.

Two Union Railways companies (South and North), responsible for Sections One and Two of CTRL, are now both owned by LCR. Union Railways (South) was previously owned by Railtrack.

Two new bridges over Midland Main Line and Thameslink railways put in place during Christmas 2002 period, to carry connection between CTRL and North London Line, and also realigned connection between East Coast Main Line and North London Line (North London Incline).

2003

February: Major realignment of Midland Main Line just north of St Pancras completed.

28 March: Last spoil removed from Stratford station below-ground box.

13 April: First limited run of Eurostar train on Section One between Westenhanger and Ashford.

19 April: Energisation of Section One overhead catenary system completed.

4 May: Bridge 111 metres long and weighing more than 9,000 tonnes is slid into place near Ebbsfleet to carry North Kent line (NKL) over CTRL. Inverted 'box' weighing 2,200 tonnes is also moved into place under NKL to carry Down-line (trains from London) connection for CTRL domestic services under NKL.

11 May: Fully instrumented Eurostar train is tested on Section One at speeds up to 220km/h (137mph).

7-8 June: First Eurostar test train runs through Ashford station on AC power.

30 July: Eurostar sets UK speed record – 334.7km/h (208mph) – on CTRL. Also in July, boring starts on two 650-metre tunnels to link East Coast Main Line and Thameslink route (work finished in April on first, cut-and-cover section of these tunnels).

5 August: CTRL Section One handed over as operational railway. First Eurostar runs full length of line, starting from Waterloo and continuing to France.

22 August: Formal handover ceremony.

16 September: Prime Minister Tony Blair officially opens Section One of CTRL. Eurostar carrying press and other guests from Waterloo runs at high speed from Fawkham Junction to Sandling; events at Waterloo, Sandling and Leeds Castle in Kent mark occasion.

21 September: Tunnelling breakthrough to Thurrock completes second of Thames tunnels.

28 September: Channel Tunnel Rail Link's Section One is opened for commercial services, cutting 20 minutes from Eurostar journey times.

4 November: 'Push-launched' Thurrock Viaduct reaches final abutment.

26 December: Bridge to connect London tunnels with King's Cross Railway Lands is successfully pushed over East Coast Main Line.

2004

27 January: First tunnelling breakthrough at London West (Gifford Street) portal next to East Coast Main Line bridge.

22 March: Final London tunnels breakthrough, into Barrington Road ventilation shaft.

9 April: St Pancras main-line station shut down.

12 April: Opening of interim Midland Main Line station on part of northern extension of St Pancras (platforms 10-13).

11 September: Further part of extension (platforms 8 and 9) opens to accommodate Thameslink services, and Thameslink route closes for construction of below-ground Thameslink station box.

13 October: Last chalk removed from tunnel beneath A2 road at Pepper Hill, near Ebbsfleet, marking completion of spoil excavations for Section Two.

22 October: Major civil engineering work for CTRL's tunnels under London completed, with last section of concrete paving laid near Stratford. Viaduct to carry realigned North London Incline (link between North London Line and East Coast Main Line) also completed in autumn 2004, together with northern span of bridge that will carry CTRL over realigned and lowered York Way.

November: Eurostar announces it will switch its entire operation to St Pancras International station in 2007, when CTRL is completed, rather than also maintaining Waterloo International station as previously envisaged. It says lower costs will result in better-value pricing for customers. Both Waterloo

The official opening of Section One of the Channel Tunnel Rail Link on 16 September 2003. Left to right are Transport Secretary Alistair Darling; London & Continental Railways Chief Executive Rob Holden; Prime Minister Tony Blair, who has been presented with a memento of the occasion; and Eurostar UK Chief Executive Richard Brown. LCR

International and North Pole depot will transfer to Department for Transport ownership as part of financial package that includes development of new Temple Mills Eurostar depot.

Eurostar says capacity at St Pancras would be maximised with six international platforms, proximity of new depot at Temple Mills, and Eurostar's established experience in train turnarounds.

Though new St Pancras area track layout provided for direct trains between CTRL and West Coast Main Line, Eurostar says there are no plans to run through international services north of London, as these would require subsidy.

2005

17 February: Progress on CTRL is demonstrated to members of International Olympic Committee, driven in convoy of Land Rovers through 'Down-line' tunnel between King's Cross and Stratford.

4 May: Thameslink box at St Pancras is completed. Through Thameslink services resume on 16 May.

6 July: London selected to host 2012 Olympic Games and Paralympic Games. CTRL domestic trains are planned to provide an 'Olympic Javelin' service, moving visitors between St Pancras, Ebbsfleet and main Games site at Stratford.

11 August: Completion of concreting of slab track in London tunnels.

First through trip from Paris to CTRL tunnel portal close to King's Cross Railway Lands is made in August by engineering test train.

2006

8 February: LCR receives go-ahead to fit out new Thameslink station below St Pancras International, to very compressed schedule, ready for services to commence in late 2007.

20 April: Construction completion ceremony at Stratford International station.

17 July: Midland Main Line services transfer to their permanent platforms (1-4) on west side of St Pancras extension.

12 September: Event to mark completion of construction of Ebbsfleet International station.

14 November: LCR announces that CTRL will now be known as High Speed 1 – 'HS1' – and will open a year later. Final track panel is put in position north of St Pancras (on Up Main Relief line).

30 November-7 December: First Eurostar train runs on Ebbsfleet to London section, hauled by diesel locomotive for tunnel ventilation tests.

2007

7 January: Energisation of overhead catenary on Ebbsfleet to St Pancras section begins.

6 March: First Eurostar train arrives at St Pancras. During March, Eurostars exceed 250km/h (155mph) during dynamic testing on Section Two.

12 June: International Olympic Committee officials are first passengers to arrive at St Pancras by Eurostar.

20 July: LCR announces handover of High Speed 1; Eurostar training and testing begin.

21 July: First Eurostars with passengers run on (almost) entire HS1 route for tunnel evacuation exercises.

St Pancras International in mid-2007, with London stretching out southwards beyond, and King's Cross station on its east side (left of picture). Eurostar trains will use St Pancras International's six central platforms, extending into the Barlow trainshed, South Eastern high-speed domestic trains to Kent will use the three eastern platforms nearest the camera, while Midland Main Line trains will use the four western platforms. LCR/URBAN EXPOSURE

4 September: Inaugural press and VIP special train achieves record-breaking run of 2hr 3min, Paris to St Pancras.

20 September: First Eurostar from Brussels to St Pancras takes 1hr 43min, a new record.

2 October: Eurostar Engineering Centre Temple Mills officially opened, as is Hitachi Rail Maintenance UK's depot at Ashford for Class 395 trains being built for high-speed domestic services.

6 November: HM The Queen inaugurates High Speed 1, and officially opens St Pancras International station.

14 November: Eurostar launches services from St Pancras International, following overnight move from Waterloo International. Eurostar journey times reduced by 15 minutes.

19 November: Eurostar begins services from Ebbsfleet International.

December: Government announces that London & Continental Railways is to be separated into three distinct businesses – infrastructure (including track and stations), land interests, and UK stake in Eurostar – and that High Speed 1 is likely to be sold in 2009.

9 December: St Pancras Thameslink station opens, with official ceremony on 10 December.

2008

9 January: Eurostar announces that 8.26 million travellers were carried in 2007, an increase of 5.1% on previous year. After launch of services from St Pancras International, between 14 November and 31 December, Eurostar sees 11% increase in passengers against same period in 2006.

HM The Queen unveiled a commemorative plaque on 6 November 2007 to mark the opening of High Speed 1. LCR/EDDIE MACDONALD

2 The CTRL route

Distances on the CTRL are measured in kilometres from St Pancras (platforms 5-7 buffer stops), with kilometre posts on the Down side of the line. The 'Up' direction is towards London. The route has reversible signalling on both tracks, although running on the left-hand track is the norm and tracks are described as 'Up' or 'Down' accordingly.

Leaving St Pancras International station, the connections from St Pancras to the North London Line (connecting to the West Coast Main Line) and East Coast Main Line diverge on the west side. The line turns east on a 250-metre-radius curve, the tightest on the CTRL, to a grade-separated junction with the domestic platform approaches and direct CTRL-North London Line route. The CTRL crosses the East Coast Main Line on a covered bridge to enter the London tunnels at the Gifford Street/London West portals, 1.5km from St Pancras.

From St Pancras to Stratford, the CTRL generally runs beneath the North London Line. Just east of the King's Cross Railway Lands, the tunnels pass only 600mm below the Fleet Sewer and major water mains at Caledonian Road, which had to be supported in a major advance works operation.

6km

The CTRL's deepest ventilation shaft, at Graham Road, Hackney, has diaphragm walls descending more than 50 metres from the surface.

9km

The line enters the Stratford station box, 1.1km long and excavated to 25 metres, accommodating Stratford International station and the junction with the line to Temple Mills depot. From Stratford to Dagenham, the CTRL tunnel route initially runs below housing but mostly below existing railways via Barking.

20km

At the eastern portal of the London tunnels near Ripple Lane, Dagenham, there is a connection to Ripple Lane yard for freight trains. The CTRL now runs on the south side of the London, Tilbury & Southend (LTS) line, mostly on piled slab across marshes.

At Dagenham the new railway reaches the Ford Motor Company site. Ford's sidings were rearranged, and there are new bridges across the CTRL, creating access to a development area.

Opposite:
The cut-and-cover tunnel at Mersham in September 2005.
LCR/Hawk Editions

28km

The CTRL crosses over to the north side of the LTS on Aveley Viaduct, as the LTS line curves south towards Purfleet.

30km

The 1.2km Thurrock Viaduct crosses the LTS line and the Dartford Tunnel exit ramps (M25 motorway northbound traffic) and passes under the QE2 bridge (M25 southbound). From a summit on the viaduct, the CTRL falls on a 1-in-40 gradient and reaches the 2.5km Thames Tunnel (entered at 32km from St Pancras). The viaduct was constructed by 'push launching' from the western end.

35km

The southern portal of the Thames Tunnel is reached, the line climbing from the tunnel at 1 in 40.

37km

At Ebbsfleet International station there is a junction leading east to the North Kent line connection, with platforms on the viaduct where trains can change over between third rail and overhead electrification.

40km

The 'Waterloo Connection' curves to make a flying junction (maximum speed 120km/h, 75mph) with the route from St Pancras at Southfleet Junction.

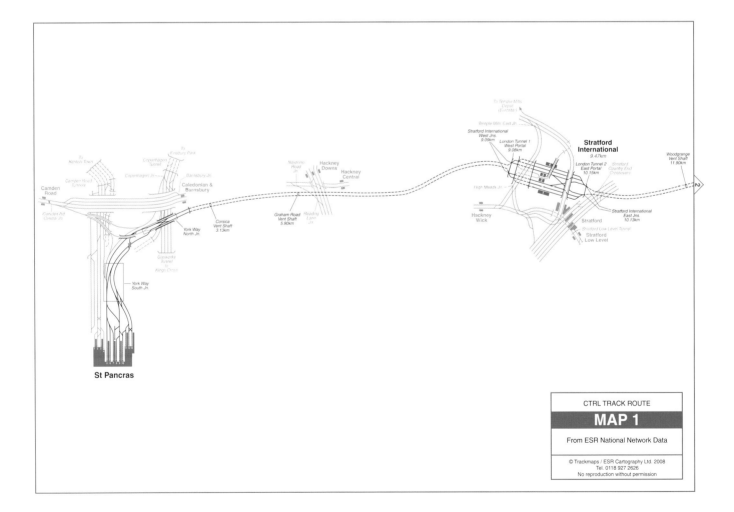

Tunnel Vision

The Waterloo Connection follows part of the former branch line to Gravesend West, diverging at Fawkham Junction from the London-Chatham main line. It was built for trains to run between the CTRL and Waterloo International via Swanley, which they did from 2003 while CTRL Section One alone was open. After the opening of the full CTRL in November 2007, the Waterloo Connection was no longer used by Eurostar trains and its future became uncertain.

The transfer from Network Rail to Channel Tunnel Rail Link ownership is near the mid-point of the 5.9km (3.7-mile) connection, with voltage changeover on the move at an electrical overlap between third rail and overhead electrification. Trains also switch from lineside signalling to cab signalling on this stretch.

The CTRL is a 300km/h (186mph) railway from here to Westenhanger (103km) on the approach to the Channel Tunnel, apart from a 270km/h (168mph) section in the Ashford area because of curvature and tunnels. (On Section Two of the CTRL, the ruling speed is 230km/h, 143mph.)

The CTRL runs on the south side of the A2/M2 for the next 14km (8.7 miles). This was a route choice made by Government in 1993, mostly keeping within the existing transport corridor, but marginally more expensive than a more direct route between here and Detling (62km) via Halling.

41km

At Singlewell there are 1.5km-long passing loops for freight, with crossovers. Passing loops are provided at about one-third and two-thirds of the full CTRL

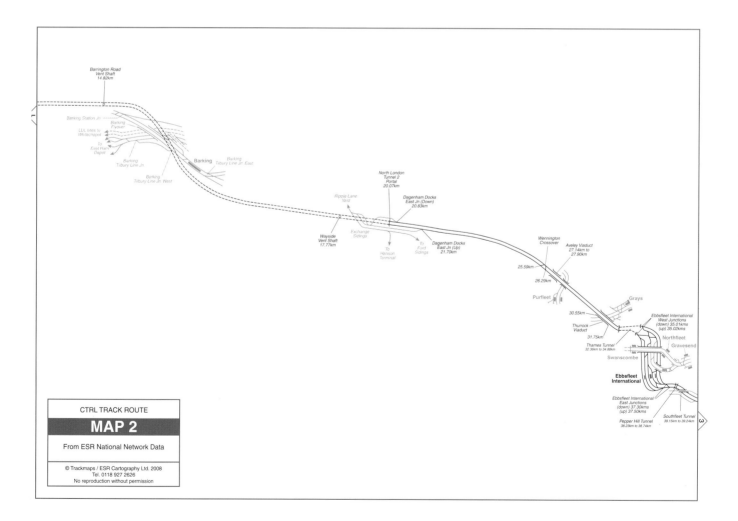

route length. Engineering sidings and a CTRL maintenance base are also here.

44km

Over the next 4km are three 'landbridges', the first at Scotland Lane, carrying parkland across the CTRL as it passes through and beside the Site of Special Scientific Interest at Ashenbank Wood, and the historic Cobham Great Park. Steep, stepped-side cuttings were also designed to reduce land taken. Resulting from an agreement with Gravesham Borough Council during Parliamentary hearings, the CTRL contributed £750,000 to the Cobham Ashenbank management scheme, aiming to conserve and improve historic, natural and landscape features with the participation of local people.

Rochester & Cobham Park golf club house was demolished and replaced further south.

47km

The new Junction 1 of the M2 motorway marks the beginning of the M2 widening project, which runs alongside and was co-ordinated with the CTRL.

49km

The CTRL is crossed by the A228, and bridges the Rochester-Swanley railway as it approaches the 1,260-metre Medway Viaduct, which itself spans the Strood-Maidstone railway.

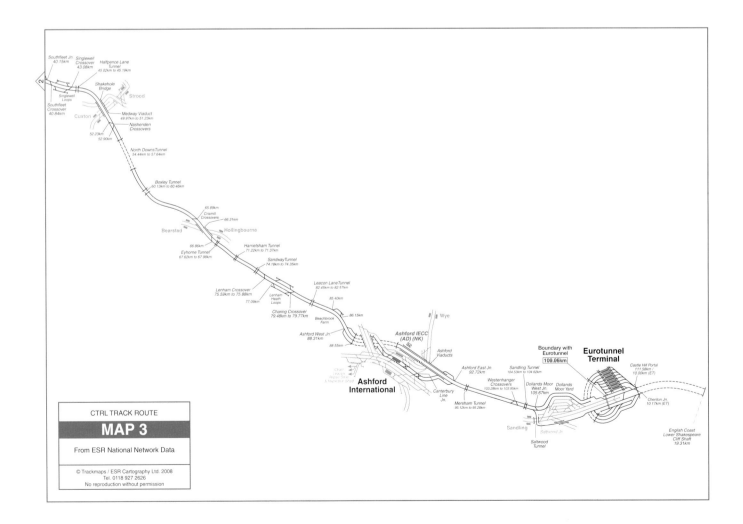

CTRL TRACK ROUTE
MAP 3
From ESR National Network Data

© Trackmaps / ESR Cartography Ltd. 2008
Tel. 0118 927 2626
No reproduction without permission

The viaduct is at the foot of gradients, and the structure was designed to withstand the forces of two passing Eurostars making emergency stops.

The approach spans of the viaduct were constructed by incremental launching of segments cast in yards on the banks. Launches took place from both banks simultaneously: investment in a second set of equipment helped recover some delays in work on the viaduct due to suspension of design work while the CTRL's funding was resolved in 1998. The easterly approach span is longer than the western one, to span a former tip for industrial waste.

The viaduct's centre span, just over 152 metres long, is of two balanced cantilevers supported on concrete islands and cast in situ.

Noise barriers are integral to the design. On the west bank is the site of the inauguration of work on the CTRL on 15 October 1998 by the Deputy Prime Minister, John Prescott.

The Medway crossing, with a Channel Tunnel-bound Eurostar on 15 October 2003. The M2 motorway widening has been completed in co-ordination with the CTRL at the Medway and in the Nashenden valley to the east.
LCR/QA PHOTOS

52km

There is a pair of crossovers at Nashenden, one of the sets of crossovers that allow the railway to operate with single-line working for engineering work. They are situated on straight sections, so are not at equal distances along the route.

54km

The 3.2km North Downs Tunnel under Blue Bell Hill, at most 100 metres below the surface, has a single 13-metre-wide, 10-metre-high bore accommodating

A Eurostar on a test run enters the southern portal of North Downs Tunnel in August 2003. LCR/QA PHOTOS

double track and walkways, with a central containment barrier.

57km

Near the southern portal of the North Downs Tunnel, an overbridge for the Pilgrims Way is wood-faced (from the point of view of walkers and riders). The ancient White Horse Stone is left undisturbed, to the east of the railway.

59km

The route through the Boxley valley runs in deep cuttings with a cut-and-cover tunnel at 60km, keeping trains out of sight in much of this area.

63km

To reduce severance of the remaining part of the ancient Horish wood, a proposed wide sloped cutting was replaced with more expensive piled walls. The CTRL joins the M20 corridor to run along the north side of the motorway.

67km

Eyhorne Tunnel is another of the cut-and-cover tunnels provided near local communities.

71km

Harrietsham Tunnel was added to the route in the Government route confirmation in January 1994.

74km

At Sandway the CTRL diverges from the motorway, which curves tightly here. The tunnel was another added in January 1994.

77km

Lenham freight loops and crossovers mark the beginning of a 270km/h maximum speed, because of curvature and tunnels, through to the west end of the cut-and-cover tunnels at Ashford.

82km

The CTRL veers north and passes through Leacon Lane Tunnel, near Westwell Leacon.

83km

The A20 road crosses over the CTRL, and the CTRL curves south again to cross the M20 motorway at a skew angle on a steel composite bridge. It then briefly runs alongside the Maidstone-Ashford railway.

85km

To the east is the site of the Beechbrook Farm CTRL construction depot, introduced when construction was phased in two sections in 1998 – the original proposed construction base at Swanscombe was on Section Two. Subsequently returned to fields, the depot was connected to the Maidstone-Ashford railway for material delivery, as well as to the CTRL.

The CTRL turns to follow a route through central Ashford with a north-westerly approach. This was agreed in April 1994 after representations by local politicians. It replaced a route alongside the M20 by-passing Ashford, though this would have had connections to Ashford International station via existing railways.

86km

The CTRL is again crossed by the A20. Here, seven buildings of a historically important Georgian model farm were dismantled and removed in what was thought to be the largest such building relocation scheme in Britain. They were moved to the South of England Rare Breeds Centre at Woodchurch, south of Ashford.

88km

Property demolition was necessary for the construction of a cut-and-cover tunnel, which takes the CTRL beneath roads and the Ashford-Maidstone railway on the west side of Ashford. Connecting lines rise on either side of the tunnel as elements of a partly grade-segregated junction, which minimises conflicts between CTRL trains calling at Ashford and trains on other routes.

A Eurostar passes Harrietsham (71km from St Pancras), bound for the Channel Tunnel in the autumn of 2003. The CTRL is in a covered way between the M20 motorway and the realigned A20 road. LCR/QA PHOTOS

90km

The main CTRL runs past Ashford International station, rising on a viaduct to cross the Ashford-Canterbury railway.

92km

Links between the station and CTRL at the east end of Ashford are grade-segregated, with the Down connection running under the viaduct to join the CTRL on the north side.

A celebrated level crossing at Aylesford Place on the existing railway was replaced by a subway; hi-tech Eurostars passing the hand-worked gates before construction of the CTRL made an incongruous sight.

The Ashford-Channel Tunnel section runs along the north side of the existing railway. For about 2km the embankments of the old and new railways are so close that support and underpinning was required.

95km

At Mersham, severed by construction of the original South Eastern Railway, a cut-and-cover tunnel encloses the new and existing lines, linking the two sides of the village. The 16th-century timber-framed Bridge House was moved 55 metres in July 2000. The 450-tonne house, supported internally and externally by concrete beams, was lifted off the ground by 15 vertical jacks and pulled by three other jacks, sliding on greased rubber and polished metal.

101km

The CTRL crosses the A20 at Grove Bridge, where the Mucky Duck pub had to be demolished.

103km

From here at Westenhanger the speed limit reduces from 300km/h, in steps of 270, 240 and 200km/h, to 160km/h at the junction with Eurotunnel.

An ornamental tunnel at Sandling, provided by the South Eastern Railway to appease a landowner, is replicated by the CTRL.

At Mersham, just east of Ashford, a cut-and-cover tunnel encloses the new and existing lines, as seen in this view from the south-east in September 2005. LCR/HAWK EDITIONS

Tunnel Vision

106km

At the approach to the Channel Tunnel, the CTRL is interlaced with the existing railway complex and motorway. The Down CTRL line (usually carrying trains towards the Channel Tunnel) goes north of the existing Saltwood Tunnel and Dollands Moor freight yard. The Up line (which displaced southwards the Network Rail line to Dover) rises from the Channel Tunnel on a seven-span, 320-metre-long, 25-metre-high viaduct along the south side of Dollands Moor yard. It crosses the top of the existing railway's Saltwood Tunnel in a cutting, about 20 metres above the existing railway.

A direct link between the CTRL and the west end of Dollands Moor yard was confirmed by the House of Commons Select Committee, giving direct access to the CTRL for the largest international rail freight vehicles – freight would otherwise have had to join the CTRL at Ashford after negotiating Saltwood Tunnel. The single-track freight link has a challenging gradient of about 1 in 40 as it climbs to run alongside the Down CTRL line.

109km

The CTRL joins Eurotunnel's railway; the Channel Tunnel portal is 111.6km from St Pancras.

The CTRL's cut-and-cover tunnel at Sandling (viewed from the west) replicates an ornamental tunnel provided on the adjacent tracks by the South Eastern Railway to appease a landowner. A Eurostar on a training run heads towards the nearby Channel Tunnel on 4 September 2003.
LCR/QA Photos

3 Building CTRL Section One

ON 15 OCTOBER 1998 DEPUTY PRIME MINISTER JOHN PRESCOTT broke the first ground in a ceremonial inauguration of work on Section One of the Channel Tunnel Rail Link (CTRL), on the banks of the River Medway near Rochester. Section One consisted of 74km (46 miles) from the Channel Tunnel to a link with the London-Chatham line at Fawkham Junction in north Kent.

Construction work on the CTRL's Medway crossing began right away, beginning with the Shakehole bridge, nearly 50km from St Pancras, which takes the CTRL over the London-Chatham railway.

An early start was also made on the North Downs Tunnel, a 3.2km (2-mile) tunnel accommodating double track and emergency walkways in a single bore. It runs under Blue Bell Hill at a maximum of 100 metres below the surface, and has a very large cross-sectional area – reckoned the largest of any rail tunnel in Europe (more than 170 square metres at maximum) – avoiding the need for pressure relief shafts into the environmentally sensitive area above. Short cut-and-cover sections were included at the portals to give a curved design with landscaping above.

With 24-hour working, the tunnel was built using excavators including 'road

Opposite:
The CTRL nears the Channel Tunnel, September 2005.

'Shotcreting' under way on 9 July 1999, as part of primary reinforcement of the North Downs Tunnel excavation during construction. A further concrete inner lining was added at a later stage. LCR/ROS ORPIN

The CTRL's route into the centre of Ashford includes a lengthy cut-and-cover tunnel. In this view looking east during the early stages of work in 1999, Ashford international and domestic station can be seen in the background. LCR/ALAN FULLER

The second motorway bridge nears completion to the north of the CTRL's Medway crossing on 27 July 2002. M2 motorway widening was carried alongside and in co-ordination with the CTRL. LCR/QA PHOTOS

Below:

The curing gantry for the waterproof membrane in North Downs Tunnel on 14 August 2000. LCR/QA PHOTOS

headers' (excavators with a rotating grinder on the end of a movable arm). A sprayed concrete lining initially provided the main support, with rock bolts and lattice arches also used; an additional reinforced concrete inner lining was added later. Much of the tunnelling spoil was used as fill for the M2 motorway widening alongside the CTRL in the Nashenden valley, just east of the Medway.

Away from these major structures, extensive earth-moving was required over a large part of Section One of the CTRL. One reason was that the route alignment selected during the Parliamentary approval process was set low in the landscape, much lower than necessary for engineering reasons, to limit environmental impact, not so much for reasons of noise as visual intrusion. 'In many places you wouldn't know it was there,' said Mike Glover, Rail Link Engineering's Technical Director in an October 2007 interview with *Modern Railways* magazine. 'You can see the train over something like 10% of the route.'

The contractors also had to build the route through relatively poor ground, as another guiding principle was to keep it within existing transport corridors as much as possible, which tend to be away from better soils preferred for habitation and agriculture. Excavating deep into weak soils, where there is also a high water table, is far from ideal – and the preference was often to squeeze the CTRL into narrow strips, for example between an existing railway and motorway, leading to extremely constrained worksites with two neighbouring routes that need to keep operating.

High-speed trains require a flat and straight route. While the CTRL was aligned to hug the M20 motorway for some distance in Kent, it has to run straighter than the motorway at its tighter curves, albeit fairly gentle as seen by car drivers. Painstaking work was also required to meet the specification for embankment earthworks to support the route, because the high-speed railway carries what Mike Glover described as 'real loads – not 25-tonne trucks, but 700-tonne trains going at 300km/h'.

TWO YEARS ON

By September 2000 the Channel Tunnel Rail Link's Section One, from the Channel Tunnel to the connection with the existing rail network in north Kent, was 40% complete. Chris Jago, Managing Director of Union Railways (South), and Railtrack's man in charge of the first phase of the CTRL, interviewed that month for *Modern Railways*, said that the national rail infrastructure company's ability to synergise between the Channel Tunnel Rail Link and national network was a big advantage – 'one zone director, one signal box, one electrical control'. Union Railways (South) was the client organisation responsible for the construction of Section One for (the then expected future owner) Railtrack. He also confirmed that the CTRL was to be a 300km/h (186mph) railway between the Channel Tunnel and Southfleet Junction, where the connection diverges to Waterloo via existing lines.

The change from the previously assumed 270km/h (168mph) speed had been made, he said, 'not to speed up point-to-point timings, but as a prudent way to deliver reliability'. The previous top speed formed a deliverable scenario, but interworking with domestic trains left Eurostars no provision for recovery from delays.

It had been hoped that domestic services could be introduced from Ashford on Section One as a pathfinder, but this was not found viable on commercial grounds, nor were spare paths available into the London area.

Roger Picard, Project Director of the Rail Link Engineering (RLE) consortium, also interviewed in September 2000, explained that the RLE joint

Southfleet Junction on 15 October 2003: in the first weeks of Eurostar services from London Waterloo International over Section One of the Channel Tunnel Rail Link, a train bound for the Channel Tunnel leaves the Waterloo Connection's flyover to join the main CTRL. The two centre tracks will join the route to St Pancras, opened in 2007.
LCR/QA Photos

venture, a consortium of the engineering shareholders of London & Continental Railways (LCR), had been formed to bring a range of complementary skills to the project: 'Systra are world leaders in high-speed design, from standards through to completion; Bechtel bring project management and also contracting expertise; and there are two prime but different UK civil engineering firms – Halcrow, whose skills include UK railway experience and unrivalled tunnelling expertise, and Arup, with special expertise in areas such as buildings and structures.'

For project delivery, Roger Picard explained that LCR adopted a multi-package construction approach to keep tight control of the project. Design and scope were set within RLE in close relationship with the client. Then, with detailed design and construction delegated to the package contractors, independent management teams focused on their own problems, with incentives for performance.

Reviewing progress on the CTRL's construction in September 2000, the most northerly contract in Section One, north Kent to the Medway, was the furthest ahead with civil engineering completion activities.

Work to provide the connection to the existing rail network at Fawkham Junction was brought forward as a contingency, in case access for infrastructure installation was not possible via the North Downs Tunnel or Medway Viaduct, but the problem did not arise. The adjacent Medway crossing and North Downs Tunnel contracts were managed together, and breakthrough of the 3.2km (2-mile) tunnel took place four months ahead of schedule on 8 June 2000, said Picard.

The Medway Viaduct had suffered some delays – design was suspended together with the whole CTRL project in early 1998, and the contractor was deprived of a planned review period when it restarted. A number of the approach piers were redesigned, and 'push launches' of the approach decks were taking place from both ends, instead of one at a time – additional investment had been made to recover time. Work on the viaduct's 152.5-metre balanced cantilever main span was about to start.

Below, left and right:

The Medway bridge under construction, in two views eastwards on 14 August 2000. The second M2 motorway bridge was to be built between the CTRL bridge and the first road bridge. 'Push launching' of bridge segments eastwards is taking place – the segments were pushed out by jacks, with new segments, added in turn at the launch site, pushing the previous segments. Bearings, sliders and pads were used to reduce friction as the segments moved across the heads of supporting piers. The girder nose attached to the first segment helped to bridge the gap, and avoided having a heavy segment leading the way.

BOTH LCR/QA PHOTOS

Tunnel Vision

*A 'pinch point' at Harrietsham (71km from St Pancras)
where the CTRL passes between the M20 motorway and the
realigned A20 road. Viewed from the east, the CTRL's
'covered way' is under construction on 15 August 2000.*
LCR/QA PHOTOS

In mid-Kent, work was 57% complete, virtually in a year from the start of
work there, but very wet weather created a quagmire in gault clay at the west end
of the area. RLE, in completing the design in close collaboration with
Hochtief/Norwest Holst, had overcome difficult ground conditions and
dewatering problems in the cut-and-cover tunnel near Boxley, one of the most
environmentally sensitive parts of the route. Its roof slab was constructed first,
then the base was to follow after dewatering the clay below. This eliminated
propping of tunnel sides.

Civils work to create the CTRL through the centre of Ashford was 55%
complete, but Ashford to the Channel Tunnel was 26% complete, the least
advanced section, after delays with land acquisition, design issues, and approvals,
as well as very significant ground condition and water-table problems.

Roger Picard recounted that (ironically in view of the problems caused earlier
in the year by rainfall) a good weather day in late August saw work stopped next
to the existing railway because of the risk of ground disturbance causing buckled
rails.

One contract on the CTRL was already finished by September 2000: the
resignalling at Ashford, let as a precursor to railway infrastructure modifications.
This changed the signal interlockings' layout, which had 'vertical' boundaries at
right angles to the tracks, dividing the station into three interlocking areas, west,
middle and east; thus a possession of all lines was required for any infrastructure
work. This preliminary contract was therefore let to change interlockings to
'semi-horizontal' boundaries. One interlocking now covered the entire south
side of the layout (broadly, the Tonbridge-Folkestone route including platforms
1 and 2). The other two enabled the Maidstone and Canterbury lines to be
controlled separately. Infrastructure modifications at Ashford embraced many

Inside North Downs Tunnel in July 2001, completed and ready for infrastructure installation. LCR

COMMISSIONING STAGES

1 factory test

2 static test after installation, using
   simulation

3 integration test under power

4 use Eurostar trains to confirm
   dynamic integration

5 test new operating procedures,
   gain approval by HM Railway
   Inspectorate, leading to permit
   to use

weekends of signalling and complex permanent way work, including installation of new routes to increase flexibility and to accommodate domestic rail traffic at existing or improved levels.

All four platforms were dual-electrified, on 'Southern Region' third-rail DC and CTRL AC overhead systems, avoiding the need for Eurostars calling at Ashford to change over between the two systems. Isolating transformers are used to prevent the CTRL's high-voltage AC inducing unwanted currents in the third-rail DC system. The Beaver Road bridge at the west end of the station was raised by about 0.5 metre to clear overhead wires, as the platforms were too close for track lowering to be possible.

Some stages of the work shifted track to enable CTRL construction, such as where the main CTRL route passed under the Maidstone line in a cut-and-cover box, allowing construction of foundations for the viaduct over the Canterbury line.

MAJOR STRUCTURES COMPLETE

Construction of Section One was more than 70% complete by October 2001 – measured by cash expended, including property purchase. Civil engineering was 85% complete, and it was on course for on-time handover to build a railway on the formation, at a cost of about £190 million.

'With construction well advanced, we're increasingly concentrating on making sure we're ready to go on Day One,' Chris Jago, Managing Director of Union Railways (South) Ltd, said in a *Modern Railways* interview.

Civil engineering work at the north end of the route was virtually finished. The Medway Viaduct's span was completed in August, and the North Downs Tunnel was also complete. The mid-Kent section was on track for completion by October, while completion of the mammoth underground and viaduct structures at the centre of Ashford was expected by January. East Kent civils work had suffered again from extreme weather, flooding much of Kent in the winter of 2000-01. The rail interfaces contract was reaching the final stages of its intricate 21-stage programme of alterations to existing infrastructure at Ashford.

The first test running of Eurostar trains was planned to begin in January 2003, with testing at up to 330km/h (205mph), 10% above the service maximum speed, expected to set a British speed record.

'We now start building the railway on the route formation, and by June 2002 all the track will be down,' said Chris Jago. 'Then there are six months for signalling installation, and Phases 2 and 3 of testing and commissioning.'

Commissioning stages would not take place sequentially – they would overlap, so that under Stage 5 emergency current isolation would need to be proved before Stage 4 introduced the trains' interaction.

Chris Jago also disclosed that while the base assumption for the domestic trains had been for a 200km/h top speed, 'we're looking at 225 or 230km/h'. The maximum London tunnels speed was 230km/h (143mph), so an equivalent capability would be valuable in minimising line occupancy.

He said, 'It seems unlikely that a train designed with the acceleration characteristics necessary to meet our existing operational assumptions would not be comfortably capable of a top speed above 200km/h.'

The change was indeed adopted, and the CTRL maximum line speeds were set at 300km/h (International Passenger), 230km/h (Domestic Passenger) and 140km/h (Freight).

The hand-operated level crossing at Willesborough, on the existing Folkestone-London railway just east of Ashford, closed on 21 April 2001, to be replaced by alternative bridge and subway routes built as part of CTRL work. With construction work on the CTRL Ashford Viaduct approaches under way on the north side, the 10.19 Paris Nord-London Waterloo International passes on 17 April 2001, formed by Class 373 Eurostar units Nos 3106/5.
BRIAN MORRISON

INFRASTRUCTURE NEARLY COMPLETE

Four years into Section One construction, in the autumn of 2002, the main junction connecting the CTRL's track to the Channel Tunnel had been installed.

Civil engineering contracts on Section One had been completed a year previously, except the Ashford to Channel Tunnel section. Work was accelerated there in the summer of 2001, and substantial completion achieved by March 2002. The infrastructure modification work at Ashford was complete.

The 'Systemwide' railway infrastructure installation work got under way on time, heading first towards the west, where the civil engineering work had been

What was described as the last major structure of Section One of the CTRL – a 372-tonne bridge crossing the M20 motorway near the Channel Tunnel – was lifted into place on the weekend of 17 July 2001, fitting into a 20-metre-wide gap between Eurotunnel's exit road and the railway already used by Eurostar and international freight trains (right of photo). The largest section lifted weighed 181 tonnes. The new bridge was to carry the CTRL 'Down' line.
LCR

completed first. With all track laid and other railway infrastructure nearly complete, some slippage compared with original target dates for commissioning was evident when Roger Picard, Project Director of Rail Link Engineering, was interviewed for *Modern Railways* in November 2002, but he was confident of meeting the opening date at the September 2003 timetable change.

At the Dollands Moor interface with Eurotunnel, a major stage of the work in October 2002 was the installation of the high-speed turnouts linking the Channel Tunnel Rail Link with the Channel Tunnel. There were three different signalling systems and three sets of signalling principles and software here – with two generations of the TVM system used by the CTRL and Eurotunnel, the latter needing to be modified. The later-generation TVM430 was also 'facing' a UK solid-state signalling interlocking for the first time.

Some overhead electrification work remained to be completed at the Channel Tunnel interface, with AC/DC immunisation requiring some track circuits to be refitted. Small transformers were being installed in power supplies, reducing cable lengths to assure electro-magnetic compatibility.

The base from which track, overhead catenary and signalling was installed was at Beechbrook Farm, completed in October 2001 on the London side of Ashford. Wedged between the Maidstone-Ashford railway and the CTRL, the site had originally been proposed as a source of material for use in earthworks, but it was not used, so contractors could get in early to prepare the site, installing an extensive railway layout over the summer of 2001. The site had a total of 14.8km (9.2 miles) of track, and included a marshalling and reception area, specialist assembly areas, and a despatch area.

Use of Beechbrook Farm was only allowed for less than a year, after which the location had to be vacated and landscaped. Work on the route was restricted to eight hours a day, five days a week, with Saturday morning in reserve.

The CTRL nears the Channel Tunnel, in a view looking eastwards in September 2005. The 'Down' and 'Up' CTRL lines run to the left and right (north and south) respectively of Dollands Moor freight yard. A connection between the CTRL and the freight yard runs alongside the Down CTRL line. The existing railway emerges from Saltwood Tunnel in the foreground. LCR/Hawk Editions

Seen here in mid-2002, Beechbrook Farm, the base for CTRL Section One infrastructure installation, was completed in October 2001 on the London side of Ashford, wedged between the Maidstone-Ashford railway (running diagonally west of the base, to the right in this photo) and the CTRL (left of photo). The location was later cleared and landscaped. LCR

At the start of a process akin to 'just in time' manufacturing, the site assembled materials arriving at night into work trains for a series of morning departures in sequence. Ballast and rails arrived by train, other materials by road.

David Bennett, RLE's Contract Manager for the 'Systemwide' rail infrastructure contracts, said in an interview for *Modern Railways* in November 2002 that the logistics of construction had, as far as possible, been carried wholesale from French high-speed lines – indeed, the overhead catenary system and track design are licensed French designs, while the signalling system followed the design used for the June 2001 opening of TGV Méditerranée. In addition, half of the staff of Section One contractors Amec Spie (and most of the field staff) were from Systra, the consultancy arm of SNCF. This should certainly give the reassurance of a known product and known performance, he commented, with 20 years of service behind it.

On average, about one week's worth of rail was on site, and 108-metre lengths delivered by train via the Channel Tunnel were flash-butt welded to 324 metres in a factory-type environment that was virtually an extension of manufacturer Krupp's Essen welding plant. The 324-metre lengths were then welded together on the route using the alumino-thermic process, a method depending much more heavily on the skills of individuals and needing quality management; because of the high geometrical standards required for high-speed railway track, flash-butt welding could not be carried out on site.

Ballast transported by ship from Glensanda on the west coast of Scotland was stockpiled on the Isle of Grain, reaching a maximum of 550,000 tonnes. Transported by train from Grain, a maximum 6,000 tonnes a day were on site at Beechbrook Farm, equivalent to four trains of 24 Autoballaster wagons. Trains were reduced to 16 vehicles for work on the CTRL. The wagons had remote hydraulic control, and could close doors against the flow of ballast.

The special requirements of a high-speed line include a high degree of cant (rail superelevation on curves), and a big shoulder of ballast up to a metre from the nearest rail. A special chute design capable of very flexible rotation was used on the wagons to meet these needs.

A single temporary track was used in building up two permanent tracks on the sub-ballast, and ballast was dropped through the tracks during a series of six or sometimes seven lifts to align the track, with around 45% of the total ballast dropped in the first lift. The ballast's memory of its original position is a vital phenomenon for the permanent way engineer to understand, said David Bennett: it will often tend to revert to a less than optimal first position.

The use at either end of the ballast trains of Class 66 locomotives with creep control, combined with the sophisticated Autoballaster wagons, was crucial to dropping ballast at a uniform rate.

Large tamping machines were used, working to very accurate vertical tolerances to assure against 'long wave' rail positioning problems. Machinery capable of lifting and lining massive pointwork was also needed, with high-speed turnouts up to 140 metres long for 160km/h (100mph) diverging speeds.

After seven lifts of the track, a dynamic track stabiliser machine passed. Up to the fourth lift, basic alignment was carried out, then two more to apply cant; these last two lifts, accounting for less than 10% of the total, were crucial to final quality. 'You can't carry out alignment adjustment in the last phases,' said David Bennett. There was 20mm tolerance at first drop, and 5mm at the end: 'It has to be done progressively, and got right, or the track will start to revert to previous levels, and dynamic effects are exaggerated.'

Sleepers are placed on the CTRL's track formation on 23 May 2002. LCR/QA Photos

Final welds were carried out at level four, then the rails were destressed, and ground to match worn-wheel profiles and provide the optimum surface. 'It is very difficult to recover rail-surface quality in the longer term if the first offering is not very good,' said David Bennett. This was a lesson learned on TGV-Nord, where more maintenance than envisaged was needed in the first few years.

High train speeds, and dynamic and wind effects make a robust installation of overhead catenary system essential. 'The quality of installation and final alignment and registration relative to the track are vital,' said David Bennett. To give even wear across trains' current-collection pantographs, a 'staggered' or offset alignment was adopted for the catenary wire, rather than running exactly parallel with the track.

One of the biggest technical issues was interaction with the adjacent Southern Region DC-electrified railways and their signalling, which drove a major immunisation and control effort against electro-magnetic interference. The CTRL's 25-0-25kV electrification is fed at 50kV and designed to high standards of immunity: the crucial tests took place during possessions of adjacent Railtrack infrastructure to check that there were no effects.

OPENING

'The Channel Tunnel Rail Link is set to open three days early,' smiled Chris Jago, MD of Union Railways (South), interviewed for *Modern Railways* shortly before the event, in September 2003. The international timetable change date of

A view from the A228 Cuxton Road bridge, just west of the Medway, on 15 October 2003 as a London-bound Eurostar passes. Major road realignment work was carried out here to accommodate the CTRL and improve roads.
LCR/QA Photos

Tunnel Vision

A London-bound Eurostar passes Sellindge (100km from St Pancras) on 15 October 2003. Here the CTRL runs through a 'pinch point' between the M20 motorway and the existing Folkestone-Ashford railway. LCR/QA PHOTOS

28 September had been adopted instead of the originally programmed opening date of 1 October.

He added that the project would be within its budget of just over £1.9 billion, though there had been major cost pressures, especially on the railway-infrastructure elements. During the construction period, technical standards had changed and, despite a policy of adopting virtually no new technology, cost estimates had been exceeded. Inflation and asset values had moved in the project's favour, however.

Chris Jago was keen to emphasise the scale of the effort devoted to opening Section One on time by those working for the contractors, Rail Link Engineering,

A Eurostar on a test run heads towards London on 8 July 2003, a few months before CTRL Section One opened; it is leaving the section where the CTRL curves to cross the M20 motorway, north of Ashford. LCR/QA PHOTOS

A Eurostar on a training run uses the connecting line from Ashford International station and heads east onto the CTRL, towards the Channel Tunnel, on 4 September 2003, a few weeks before CTRL Section One opened.
LCR/QA PHOTOS

and client Union Railways, as well as many other partners including Network Rail, Eurostar, and the Kent passenger train operating company, Connex.

It was no secret that intensive work had been required in recent months to achieve the CTRL's opening, with signalling and electrical supply issues among those to be resolved. Phase 4 of commissioning – dynamic testing of the wheel/rail interface – slipped by several months. Phase 5 moved the process into 'operations mode' – testing systems and procedures, and offering hands-on experience for signallers and engineers on such things as how to set up a track possession, or evacuate a train, including in a tunnel or on a viaduct. At the handover from Phase 4 to 5, a completion handover certificate (CHOC) invoked the safety case and CTRL rule book.

CTRL safety case acceptance was achieved on 5 August, but 'CHOC' did not take place until 22 August. This did not prevent Eurostar driver familiarisation from starting, but major difficulties were posed as about two-thirds of Eurostar drivers were French, and training was starting early in the August holiday period in France.

The official opening of Section One of the Channel Tunnel Rail Link. Transport Secretary Alistair Darling stands between two Eurostars at Sandling, close to the Channel Tunnel, on 16 September 2003. LCR

A Eurostar heads for London, climbing away from the Channel Tunnel on the 'Up' line at the start of the CTRL in October 2003. LCR/QA PHOTOS

On 29 August, 28 days ahead of the opening date, the CTRL team applied to the Government's Project Representative for the Permit to Use. In effect, this is Government certification that the grant has been spent as expected, that undertakings and assurances given during the Parliamentary process have been met or mitigated – but especially that the railway meets the criteria of safety, speeds, headways and so on that had been set.

With the opening of Section One of the CTRL, Eurostar journey times were reduced by 20 minutes, with fastest timings of about 2hr 35min London-Paris and 2hr 20min London-Brussels (a 2hr 15min Brussels-London train was introduced in 2004).

A new company, Network Rail CTRL Ltd, would now manage the railway,

A London-bound Eurostar crosses the Medway Viaduct on 7 November 2003. LCR/QA PHOTOS

A view of the Medway from above the east bank on 29 September 2005 with a Eurostar train crossing.
LCR/HAWK EDITIONS

Below:
Ashford: the main CTRL climbs from a cutting (it passes beneath the Maidstone line west of the station) onto a viaduct (to cross the Canterbury line) as it passes the north side of the station. To the north side of the viaduct in this September 2005 view is the site of the depot for the Hitachi-built Class 395 Kent express trains, opened in 2007.
LCR/HAWK EDITIONS

and an operations and maintenance organisation went live with the award of the Permit to Use. It included some 45 people including civil, electrical and other specialist engineers, a contracts manager, and a strategic planning manager. This last post was crucial to maintenance and operation, as the CTRL will not have any 28- or 52-hour possessions – 'all blockades will be for 7 hours, and we will never renew this railway again,' said Chris Jago. Instead, ballast, sleepers and rail

A view along the CTRL at Ashford, eastwards towards the Channel Tunnel, in September 2005. The cut-and-cover tunnel in the foreground encloses connecting lines between the CTRL and the international station. LCR/HAWK EDITIONS

would be replaced in sequence, so a highly disciplined organisation would be required, with a very quick method of taking and giving up possessions, requiring just 1 minute by automated procedures.

The TVM signalling system has its own continuous monitoring of voltage and current in all track circuits, for early warning of problems. Comprehensive lineside vehicle monitoring is also provided, to spot problems such as hot axles.

By December 2004 Union Railways was able to report that Section One of the CTRL, then more than a year old, had run very reliably and smoothly. Eurostar delay attributed to CTRL infrastructure averaged about 11 seconds per train, 'so this seems to squash any idea that Section One was finished in a hurry and would be unreliable,' said Union Railways' Alan Dyke. By May 2006 the average delay to services on Section One was 7.5 seconds per train – it did drop to 5 seconds, until a single incident occurred to push up the average.

4 Building CTRL Section Two

B Y SEPTEMBER 2000 WALT BELL, Managing Director of Union Railways (North) and former Bechtel senior vice-president, was able to report a major effort to start the principal contracts for CTRL Section Two in July 2001. Section Two was half the length of Section One, but was expected to cost 50% more, he pointed out. It had the majority of the stations, greater operational and development opportunities, attracted the greater share of Government subsidy, domestic train operations came into the picture – and there was the little matter of St Pancras station.

Unlike much of the first section, Section Two runs through a heavily urbanised area with many neighbours. 'There is an environmental impact here

Opposite:
Creating the eastern part of the St Pancras deck extension in October 2003. LCR/HAWK EDITIONS

The Channel Tunnel Rail Link track layout and associated works, overlaid on an aerial view of the area around St Pancras as it was before CTRL construction began. The orange lines show the Thameslink route; the below-ground Thameslink station box is outlined in yellow, showing how it underlies much of the St Pancras station extension, shown in red, so had to be built first. LCR

also, though of a different kind,' said Walt Bell in an interview for *Modern Railways*. Were the major items of engineering on Section Two especially innovative? The long tunnels under London would be a big effort because of the sheer amount of work, said Walt Bell, but the ground conditions were quite well known – they had been tunnelled regularly. The Thames tunnels, which had to be bored through chalk, were likely to be more difficult than the London tunnels – a slurry-pressurised tunnelling head had been chosen for the wet chalk.

As for the CTRL's London terminus at St Pancras, the structural, architectural and engineering work did not require any unique technology, he said, but the job would take twice as long as it might because the station and railway had to be kept running throughout, and there was complex co-ordination with improvement of the cross-London Thameslink railway, and the London Underground.

The St Pancras work was the most critical item in the Section Two programme, he believed. The Thames Tunnel drive could have presented programme risk, but a back-up machine was decided on, and the plan to have one railhead just south of the Thames for infrastructure installation had also been amended to provide a second base north of the river in the Ripple Lane, Dagenham, area.

'It is a tenet of this project not to experiment.' said Walt Bell. 'It's already huge, with a price already near £6 billion, and a tight timetable. The signalling system, track and power specifications are conservative – proven technology, aimed at getting finished as soon as possible.'

For railway infrastructure installation on Section Two, a base next to the south side of the Thames at Ebbsfleet was to be used, for the stretch including Ebbsfleet station, the Thames Tunnel, and a combination of viaduct over the Dartford road crossing approaches and piled slab across Rainham marshes. The further base at Ripple Lane would supply contracts for slab track, overhead catenary and signalling through the tunnels into St Pancras.

FULL TILT

Interviewed again a year later, in October 2001, Walt Bell was able to report that Section Two was 'going full tilt'. The beginning of 2002 was to see all main civil engineering contracts for Section Two in place – committing about 78% of the value.

Work was under way on the longest-duration contracts. The contractors for the 18km (11 miles) of twin tunnels, from Dagenham to the King's Cross Railway Lands on the approach to St Pancras, were on site. At Stratford, the diaphragm walls of a station box (eventually to be 1 kilometre long, 50 metres wide and 25 metres deep) were beginning to take shape.

Tunnelling contractors were first concentrating on the five London tunnel ventilation shafts, and on preliminary work for the tunnel portals on the approach to St Pancras and at the country end of the tunnels at Ripple Lane.

The Thames Tunnel contractor had also fully mobilised at the south side. The Thames tunnels were to use what Walt Bell described with a smile as 'one and a half' tunnelling machines – the 'half' consisting of a set of the critical parts of the machine, bearings, motors and so on, together with other long-lead-time items. The machine would first bore the Down line from the south to Thurrock ('Up' in CTRL parlance is towards London), with slurry pumped through the tunnel. The machine would then be dismantled, returned to the south side and rebuilt

Tunnelling for the CTRL Thames tunnels is inaugurated by Walt Bell, Managing Director, Union Railways (North), on 11 July 2002. LCR/QA Photos

as needed from the spare kit of parts, before driving the Up tunnel. This scheme had been adopted because of the lack of a suitable worksite or disposal area on the north side of the river.

The London tunnels would have three headings in progress simultaneously. The tunnel boring machines excavated 8.15-metre-diameter tunnels, which, with concrete lining, resulted in 7.15-metre-diameter running tunnels. The tunnels ran mostly through clay and sands, with dewatering necessary where they dipped below the water table.

From Stratford to St Pancras two machines would work on the twin bores, generally running beneath the North London Line, with one machine driving a few hundred metres ahead of the other. These earth-pressure-balance machines would emerge after 7.5km (4.7 miles), just east of the East Coast Main Line. The CTRL would then cross the East Coast Main Line on a bridge into the King's Cross Railway Lands. Spoil from these tunnels would be conveyed to Stratford and deposited onto the railway lands there, raising most of the area by 6 to 9

The Up-line tunnelling machine for the Stratford-St Pancras section is assembled at the west end of the Stratford station box on 25 July 2002. LCR/QA PHOTOS

The bridge to take the CTRL across the East Coast Main Line into the King's Cross Railway Lands takes shape on 3 October 2003, in advance of its installation at Christmas of that year. LCR/CHRIS HENDERSON

The bridge to take the CTRL across the East Coast Main Line into the King's Cross Railway Lands is slid into place on Christmas Day 2003. BOTH LCR/URBAN EXPOSURE

A view from above the London West Tunnel portal into the enclosed bridge across the East Coast Main Line on 23 January 2004. The intervening section of the CTRL was later covered over. LCR

metres after the spoil has been compacted. This would raise the land above the River Lea flood plain, easing redevelopment: the station box itself was expected to need permanent dewatering equipment.

Tunnelling for 5km (3.1 miles) from Stratford to the east, mostly beneath houses, would finish at the Barrington Road ventilation shaft, in East Ham. Again, two machines would be used on the twin bores, with spoil conveyed to Stratford. Two more machines would drive 5.5km west to Barrington Road from

the country portal of the London tunnels at Ripple Lane, beneath the existing railway through Barking. Machines from the two contracts would be dismantled at Barrington Road. Spoil from the easternmost section would be conveyed to Ripple Lane, with some to be used on the route across the marshes to the east. With this section having its own tunnel-lining-segment plant at Ripple Lane, the need to transport 3-tonne segments would be avoided.

Walt Bell said, 'The tunnels make up a huge item, but they're less critical than St Pancras – it's enormously complicated, and keeping the station operating during the rebuilding really complicates it.'

Both the big civils contracts at St Pancras (on the railway lands and deck extension/Thameslink box contracts) were under way: the second of five gasholders to come down had gone in September 2001.

The London tunnels, reaching more than 30 metres below ground, were to have slab track, and a running speed of 230km/h (143mph), reducing to 80km/h (50mph) at the St Pancras approach. Normally, the tunnels were to be ventilated by the passage of trains. In case of a major incident, passengers would evacuate via cross passages to the other tunnel, with air flow controlled using fans in the London tunnels' five ventilation shafts. The shafts were not intended for evacuation.

For the London tunnels, in the event of fire, plans were for a 'safe haven' to be created in the non-incident tunnel, enabling passengers to cross into a smoke-free atmosphere. This would be achieved by means of large fans in the vent shafts with jet fans mounted in the tunnel at the portals.

The Saccardo system would also be used for the Thames Tunnel:

Tunnel lining segments are loaded onto a construction train at the south side of the Thames tunnels on 2 September 2002. LCR

The Down-line tunnelling machine breaks through to reach Barrington Road shaft on 3 December 2003 after driving east from Stratford. LCR/QA Photos

Street-level buildings were cleared from the west side of
St Pancras station before the Thameslink station box,
which would lie below the road and the western part
of the station's extension, could be built. The eastern part
of the extension can be seen under construction behind the
Midland Mainline train in the station in this 17 December
2003 photo. LCR/URBAN EXPOSURE

this comprises powerful fans injecting air through large nozzles at each portal,
thus raising air pressure in the non-incident tunnel to create a 'safe haven'.
Smoke control could be obtained by using fans at one portal only.

ST PANCRAS DESIGN

Accommodating 400-metre-long Eurostars at St Pancras meant extending the
platforms by some 200 metres to the north, with the extension widened to the
west for Midland Main Line inter-city trains, and to the east for domestic express
trains using the CTRL to achieve fast journeys from and to Kent.

In the rebuilt station, early plans saw Midland Main Line (MML) trains
having one very long platform extending right back into the existing trainshed,
and three platforms on its west side. The Eurostar departure lounge was to be at
platform level on the west side, with access to the international platforms via a
footbridge. Arriving passengers would leave via a new concourse below the
platforms at the north end of the William Barlow-designed trainshed.

The plan was subsequently revised, avoiding Eurostar's departing passengers
having to use a total of three levels, and dispensing with intrusive access bridges
in the main trainshed for the international platforms, as well as banishing diesel
trains and their fumes from the trainshed.

The buffer stops for all four MML platforms would now lie north of the
trainshed, on the west side, giving a single concourse. In place of the long MML
platform, large slots would be cut into the station deck on the west side, creating
a two-level space and providing for transfer between levels. Three platforms for
the Kent expresses would be on the east side of the extension.

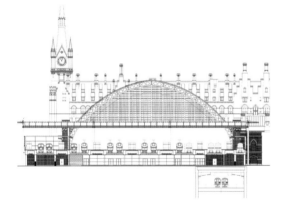

A cross-section of the rebuilt St Pancras station, north of the
Barlow trainshed. The Eurostar platforms are in the middle,
Midland Main Line platforms to the right (west), with
Thameslink below; and Kent express platforms on the left.
LCR

Most pedestrian circulation would be at street level, from which people would
go up to most platforms and platform-level retail outlets, or down to the
Thameslink platforms, in a new station beneath Midland Road and the west side
of St Pancras. Under the front of the station would be London Underground's
new western ticket hall, giving direct access to the sub-surface lines.

For international departures and arrivals, all the facilities would be
immediately under the trains, in the station's undercroft, with moving walkway
links up to the platforms.

Opposite, top:
A plan of St Pancras at undercroft level. LCR

Opposite, bottom:
A plan of St Pancras at platform level. LCR

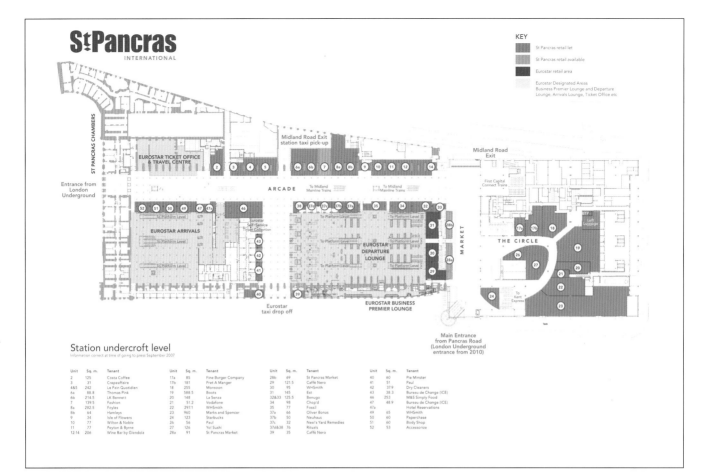

St Pancras INTERNATIONAL

St Pancras Chambers

Entrance from London Underground

Midland Road Exit station taxi pick-up

Midland Road Exit

EUROSTAR TICKET OFFICE & TRAVEL CENTRE

ARCADE

To Midland Mainline Trains

To Midland Mainline Trains

First Capital Connect Trains

EUROSTAR ARRIVALS

Eurostar Self-Service Ticket Collection

To Platform Level

To Platform Level

To Platform Level

EUROSTAR DEPARTURE LOUNGE

To Platform Level

To Platform Level

To Platform Level

MARKET

THE CIRCLE

Left Luggage

To Kent Express

Eurostar taxi drop off

EUROSTAR BUSINESS PREMIER LOUNGE

Main Entrance from Pancras Road (London Underground entrance from 2010)

KEY
- St Pancras retail let
- St Pancras retail available
- Eurostar retail area
- Eurostar Designated Areas Business Premier Lounge and Departure Lounge, Arrivals Lounge, Ticket Office etc

Station undercroft level
Information correct at time of going to press September 2007

Unit	Sq. m.	Tenant	Unit	Sq. m.	Tenant	Unit	Sq. m.	Tenant	Unit	Sq. m.	Tenant
2	125	Costa Coffee	17a	85	Fine Burger Company	28b	69	St Pancras Market	40	60	Pie Minster
3	31	Crepeaffaire	17b	181	Pret A Manger	29	121.5	Caffè Nero	41	51	Paul
4&5	242	Le Pain Quotidien	18	255	Monsoon	30	95	WHSmith	42	37.9	Dry Cleaners
6a	88.8	Thomas Pink	19	588.5	Boots	31	145	Est	43	38.3	Bureau de Change (ICE)
6b	214.5	LK Bennett	20	148	La Senza	32&33	125.5	Benugo	46	253	M&S Simply Food
7	139.5	Fashion	21	51.2	Vodafone	34	98	Chop'd	47	48.9	Bureau de Change (ICE)
8a	282.5	Foyles	22	297.1	WHSmith	35	77	Fossil	47a		Hotel Reservations
8b	64	Hamleys	23	960	Marks and Spencer	37a	66	Oliver Bonas	49	65	WHSmith
9	34	Isle of Flowers	24	123	Starbucks	37b	50	Neuhaus	50	60	Paperchase
10	77	Wilton & Noble	26	56	Paul	37c	32	Neal's Yard Remedies	51	60	Body Shop
11	77	Peyton & Byrne	27	126	Yo! Sushi	37d&38	76	Rituals	52	53	Accessorize
12-14	206	Wine Bar by Glendola	28a	91	St Pancras Market	39	35	Caffè Nero			

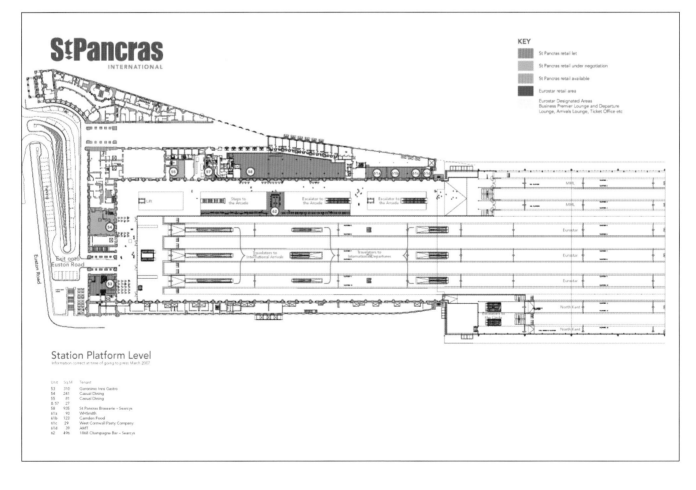

St Pancras INTERNATIONAL

Euston Road

Exit onto Euston Road

Lift

Steps to the Arcade

Escalator to the Arcade

Escalator to the Arcade

MML

MML

Travelators to International Arrivals

Travelators to International Departures

Eurostar

Eurostar

Eurostar

North Kent

North Kent

KEY
- St Pancras retail let
- St Pancras retail under negotiation
- St Pancras retail available
- Eurostar retail area
- Eurostar Designated Areas Business Premier Lounge and Departure Lounge, Arrivals Lounge, Ticket Office etc

Station Platform Level
Information correct at time of going to press March 2007

Unit	Sq.M	Tenant
53	310	Geronimo Inns Gastro
54	241	Casual Dining
55	81	Casual Dining
& 57	27	
58	935	St Pancras Brasserie – Searcys
61a	93	WHSmith
61b	123	Camden Food
61c	29	West Cornwall Pasty Company
61d	39	AMT
62	496	1868 Champagne Bar – Searcys

Work is in progress to create the eastern part of the St Pancras deck extension in October 2003. Midland Mainline trains were still using the St Pancras trainshed, reaching it via a temporary route alignment. LCR/HAWK EDITIONS

The new roof over the extended platforms was set at the level of the screen at the north gable of the existing St Pancras trainshed. The extension roof is an aluminium-clad louvre-blade and glass structure, carried about 20 metres above the street on slender pillars. A 4.5-metre brim is provided to help keep out the weather, though full enclosure was ruled out by the presence of Midland Main Line diesel trains.

A new transept in the middle of the new station – at undercroft level below the north gable of the trainshed – put new main entrances at east and west ends, with, at the west end, the entrance down to the new Thameslink platforms.

A major new additional Underground entrance and northern ticket hall was to be built near the east entrance (and on the western side of King's Cross main-line station) with new escalators down to the ends of the Victoria, Northern and Piccadilly Line platforms not served by the existing escalators. (This remained under construction when St Pancras International opened in 2007, after delays in gaining Government authority.)

By December 2002 the scale of the new CTRL terminal and its approaches was clearly evident. Columns for the first, eastern, part of the St Pancras extension deck were going up; preparations were well under way for new Thameslink-route tunnel connections across the King's Cross Railway Lands to the East Coast Main Line; and girder bridges were nearly complete, ready to be launched across the Midland Main Line at Christmas 2002. These would carry the CTRL's North London Line (NLL) link and a revised connection between the East Coast Main Line and the NLL.

LARGE-SCALE WORKS

Interviewed for *Modern Railways* in September 2003, Alan Dyke, then Managing Director of Union Railways (North), was able to say, 'Section Two of the CTRL is now at maximum output, and the scale of work can now be seen.'

Section Two was more than 50% complete. Just beyond the junction with Section One at Southfleet Junction, a 500-metre cut-and-cover tunnel was under construction to take the CTRL under the A2 road and north into the Ebbsfleet valley.

'You quickly run out of adjectives to describe the scale of works at several of the major locations in Section Two,' said Alan Dyke.

The bridge to carry the North Kent railway over the CTRL was reckoned one of the largest bridges ever to be slid into place in the UK, at 111 metres long, with three spans and a weight or more than 9,000 tonnes. It was constructed 50 metres north of its final position, and eight 3-metre-diameter tunnels were dug under the existing railway to enable the 'slide track' and permanent foundation for the bridge to be constructed in advance. The bridge was put in place over the 2003 May Day holiday weekend; 23 hours of excavation took place to remove the North Kent line (NKL) embankment; then the bridge was lifted on 30 hydraulic jacks and pushed into final position over 6 hours.

In a second operation, a concrete tunnel was jacked on to trailers and driven into position. The 2,200-tonne structure – 60 metres long, 8 metres high and 6.5 metres wide – would take the connection for Kent-bound CTRL domestic services under the NKL. Around 10,000 cubic metres of chalk were excavated from the existing railway embankment to make way.

'This was a major achievement, in an operation of high complexity and risk,' said Alan Dyke. 'The NKL box itself is a major achievement, but it was overshadowed by the larger bridge slide.'

Moving north from Ebbsfleet, the second drive of the twin-bore Thames Tunnel was soon to break through, ahead of programme. The tunnel represented a critical risk, because the railhead for rail infrastructure installation north of the Thames was to be at Ebbsfleet, south of the Thames. 'Problems with a jammed tunnelling machine, water ingress or finding flint in the way of the tunnel drive were far from inconceivable,' said Alan Dyke.

Thurrock Viaduct on the north side of the Thames was a very high-profile piece of work, with a long approach 'spearing' under the QE2 Dartford Crossing bridge, gradually constructed from one end. It had crossed the London, Tilbury

The major bridge slide near Ebbsfleet involved a bridge 111 metres long and weighing more than 9,000 tonnes being slid into place on 3 May 2003 to carry the North Kent line over the CTRL. LCR/QA Photos

A view eastwards along Thurrock Viaduct towards the Thames Tunnel on 12 July 2004, with the QE2 Dartford crossing bridge in the background. LCR/QA Photos

Building CTRL Section Two

The Thurrock Viaduct, being pushed eastwards towards the Thames Tunnel on 1 May 2003, has reached its crossing of the former London, Tilbury & Southend Railway just on the London side of the M25 motorway Dartford crossings, about 31km from St Pancras. LCR/QA Photos

& Southend (LTS) railway and the exit ramps from the Dartford road tunnels, and was heading under the QE2 bridge using the system of 'push launches' also seen at the Medway Viaduct on Section One. Car drivers emerging from the Dartford tunnels see only a slab of concrete well above them – trains are hidden at the requirement of highway authorities.

After another viaduct near Purfleet, the CTRL continues across Rainham and Aveley marshes, 'carried, in effect, on 7km of viaduct sitting on the ground,' says Alan Dyke. 'It was built using piled slab construction – the stable slab would carry high-speed trains from day one, rather than having perhaps five years of speed restrictions with an embankment.'

Piling work was close to completion by September 2003, but a serious incident occurred here in spring 2003: a piling rig fell at the side of the Aveley Viaduct west of Purfleet, where the CTRL crosses the LTS. Used to create piled abutments, the continuous flight auger rig was the largest of its kind, 35 metres high and carried on a crawler base. It had worked safely for several weeks until obstructions were met by the rig. These were excavated by other plant, and the problem arose with backfilling, which was not sufficiently consolidated and reinforced, causing the rig to sink slowly and fall across the LTS tracks.

The London tunnels were more than half way to the completion of overall construction. 'There have been learning curves to negotiate, and teething troubles with the machines, but all the drives are above predicted average performance. The result has been good-quality tunnels, on line and level, in programme and within budget,' said Alan Dyke.

However, at Lavender Street near Stratford in February 2003 a machine driving east hit an unexpected and uncharted void, suspected to be related to back-garden wells. The ground was stabilised overnight, the gardens were later restored and structural work was needed at one property. Ex gratia payments were made.

'Other evidence of tunnelling has been restricted to the rumbling of narrow gauge construction trains in the tunnels,' says Alan Dyke, 'and ground settlement has been nowhere near predictions.' The figure achieved had been half of one per cent – four times better than the case stated in consultation. The predicted levels of settlement would have meant significant problems for utility companies, which would have to be rectified at the CTRL project's expense.

As the CTRL approaches the Stratford station area, heading west, it runs relatively close to the surface, and here tunnelling machines passed within five metres of the London Underground Central Line tunnels without incident. Surveying and monitoring of the tunnel condition was established, to the extent

Above and above left:
The concrete deck of the Thurrock Viaduct was edged over the Dartford Tunnel exit road and beneath the QE2 bridge at night while road traffic was diverted. All LCR/ROS ORPIN

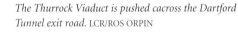

The Thurrock Viaduct is pushed cacross the Dartford Tunnel exit road. LCR/ROS ORPIN

The Thurrock Viaduct is pushed close to its final position on 30 October 2003. LCR/QA Photos

that the surrounding clay could be seen to compress with trains in the tunnels in the rush hour, then recover.

The five ventilation shafts for the London tunnels, which not only bring air to the tunnels but also allow emergency access, and are also the site of equipment rooms, were all constructed by September 2003, and fitting-out was to start shortly.

At Stratford, the station box was complete, as was the station slab. 'You can describe a huge space 1 kilometre long, 50 metres wide and 20 metres deep, but you can't really conceive its size without seeing it,' said Alan Dyke. 'A huge extent of diaphragm walling and slab has been constructed without incident, and the London tunnels are being driven from the box, giving ample space to work from – which is quite unlike previous London tunnelling sites.' The 2 million or so cubic metres of spoil were being used in a land raise operation around the Stratford Railway Lands, helping to enable regeneration of the contaminated and largely derelict area.

At St Pancras it was hard to over-state the challenge of building a major new station while the Midland Main Line train company continued to operate trains, said Alan Dyke. 'It's really the equivalent of five new stations,' he said. 'First comes the four-platform interim station on the east side of the new northern extension deck, where Midland Main Line will move next Easter.

'Ignoring the new Thameslink station for a moment, that will enable work to start on the existing St Pancras station, allowing access to the trainshed to repair and renovate the roof. It will have new cladding and will be restored to its

original splendour. The platforms will be rebuilt and a further part of the deck extension reaching 200 metres to the north will be constructed.

'The third step will be to build four platforms on the west side of the new deck, creating the final location for Midland Main Line trains – that will be the second station opening.

'Next the international platforms will be constructed in the middle, and the CTRL domestic platforms to the east side – two more new stations.'

The fifth station would be the new one for Thameslink trains under Midland Road and the west side of St Pancras.

INTO THE TRAINSHED

By December 2004 there was a continuous route from London St Pancras all the way to the junction with Section One of the CTRL in north Kent, on which the first track was being laid.

Major civil engineering for the tunnels under London was completed ahead of schedule, with the last section of concrete paving laid in late October 2004. The end of tunnel boring had been marked by an event at Stratford in March 2004.

Further high-profile and critical milestones for the project in 2004 were the opening of the interim Midland Main Line station at Easter and its extension to accommodate Thameslink services in September. Alan Dyke, Managing Director of Union Railways (North), said in a *Modern Railways* interview, 'It was quite a

The eastern part of the St Pancras extension nears completion on 18 January 2004. Midland Mainline trains would move to an interim station here in April 2004, to enable work to go ahead in the St Pancras trainshed, and on the Thameslink box, below ground level at the station's west side. LCR

Work is ongoing to complete the interim station in the eastern part of the St Pancras extension on 11 March 2004. LCR/QA Photos

On 9 April 2004 the 23.40 to Derby became the last train to leave St Pancras before work began in earnest to convert the trainshed for its new role. LCR/Urban Exposure

Looking south over the Barlow trainshed roof at St Pancras in August 2005: the ribs of the roof have been painted blue and, supported by the ribs, new 'ridge and furrow' glazing panels are being installed, with slate (from the same quarry used in the original 1860s construction) lower down on the flanks of the roof. LCR/Urban Exposure

complex activity to shut down St Pancras main-line station on Friday night and open again on the Monday morning on the new deck – having commissioned track, signalling, passenger information systems and so on over the Easter weekend.

'It's indicative of the complexity of the work at St Pancras that it took us, from the start of work in July 2001, until Easter 2004 to start on the trainshed – because we had to relocate track several times over, to create the new Midland Main Line approaches, build the deck extension, and move the trains out.'

A visit to the trainshed in late November 2004 found the station platforms being removed, and the first reinforcement mesh being placed for the new cast concrete deck on top of the original station-level deck. About 1,400 workers were on site at St Pancras and its approaches.

A movable scaffold had been installed within the Barlow-designed trainshed for work on the roof, which would see existing materials completely replaced with new glazing panels and slates. A 70-metre scaffold span was made up of aluminium trusses with steel sheeting, providing a run-off for cleaning water, a safety screen, and weather protection. It was to be lowered and re-erected in different positions. The roof itself was temporarily pierced by cranes.

Meanwhile, in the undercroft, the painstaking work of restoring the slender cast-iron columns that support the station deck was under way – very careful shot-blasting was needed because of the presence of lead in the old paint. The undercroft base was being lowered to accommodate the services for the station and the retail facilities that the area would house: a supported floor would be installed above.

There was an unexpected need for extensive work on the columns. As they were made of cast iron and seated on granite blocks, they took a downwards load well, but could not be expected to take significant lateral loads, explained Ailie MacAdam, Project Director of Rail Link Engineering, in an October 2007 interview for *Modern Railways*. 'So we had to add a bearing on the top of every column. We came up with a way of getting the bearings "poured in" together with the concrete deck, so it didn't hold up progress.'

There was also a very large construction site right underneath where the pointwork giving access to the St Pancras platforms had been – here the new station 'box' structure for Thameslink was being built around the existing Thameslink tunnels, under Midland Road on the west side of the St Pancras terminus. Cross-London Thameslink services were suspended from 11 September 2004. This was later than originally planned, partly because earlier work north of St Pancras, near St Pancras graveyard, resulted in the discovery of many more bodies than anticipated, and a period of sensitive collaboration with the Church of England and specialist contractors followed, to remove and re-inter the bodies.

'It's difficult to visualise, even when visiting the site, the impact of the Thameslink box underneath the station,' said Alan Dyke in the December 2004 interview. 'You can't really see much, as it's below ground, and even the way we're building it, from the top down (putting the roof in first), helps to obscure the scale of the work.'

Despite differences over working hours, Alan Dyke said, 'I'm pleased to say we

The spacing between the cast-iron columns in the St Pancras station undercroft was determined by the dimensions of beer barrels, which came by train from Burton upon Trent and were stored here. The granite footings can be seen in this photograph taken on 4 July 2003. Raised flooring was later installed and bearings provided on top of the columns to protect them from altered lateral forces in the rebuilt station. LCR/Urban Exposure

The eastern part of the St Pancras station extension is accommodating Midland Mainline and Thameslink trains in October 2004 as work goes on to build the Thameslink station box, which will partly lie below the extension on the west side. LCR/HAWK EDITIONS

Opposite, top:
Work in progress to create the Thameslink box on 19 November 2004 – a southward view. The neighbouring tunnel section can be seen in the background. LCR/URBAN EXPOSURE

do have good relationships with our neighbours, the local residents, and because of that we've actually been able to ease some of the restraints on working. So we have been working underground for 24 hours a day, though not taking material away at night – preparatory work including some demolition in the excavation has been permitted overnight.'

The piled sidewalls and much of the roof of the station box had been put in place in advance of breaking up the existing tunnel. Construction of the Thameslink box was completed in May 2005.

Reviewing progress along the Section Two route, Alan Dyke said, 'The finished Thames tunnels have had fans fitted, the track and cables are in place. With tracklaying now continuing north of the Thames tunnels, long welded rail strings delivered to Ripple Lane, Dagenham, are being pulled into the London tunnels.'

The CTRL's Thurrock Viaduct was finished, and tracklaying began there in late 2004. Just before that, a public walk across the structure took place in early November, taking advantage of the asphalt finish over the waterproofing on the 1.3km viaduct. The walk was advertised locally, and attracted about 700 people on a dry Sunday, continuing part of the way into the Thames Tunnel as far as tracklaying activity permitted.

The route across the Rainham and Aveley marshes – 7km of 'viaduct on the ground' – was also complete, and worksite areas were gradually being returned to nature.

Final overhead line electrification work is in progress in the Thameslink box at St Pancras on 27 April 2005.
LCR/URBAN EXPOSURE

Left:
Inside the completed Thameslink below-ground station box at St Pancras on 27 April 2005 – fitting-out was to be authorised later. LCR/URBAN EXPOSURE

The CTRL formation is in place across the Rainham and Aveley marshes in October 2004. The CTRL crosses from south to north of the London, Tilbury & Southend line at Aveley Viaduct as it heads east towards the Thames Tunnel.
LCR/Hawk Editions

Below:
Ebbsfleet station and surrounding CTRL infrastructure under construction, as seen in a view northwards towards the Thames Tunnel in October 2004. LCR/Hawk Editions

Tunnel Vision

Where the route neared the London tunnels, another critical item, the railway works at Ripple Lane, were completed in September 2004. Three Exchange Sidings have connections to the CTRL and London, Tilbury & Southend route, with Ford and other rail freight traffic directed through them. 'This is a strategic piece of infrastructure,' said Alan Dyke, 'enabling freight serving London to join/leave the CTRL, and also providing a refuge for CTRL trains that cannot enter the London tunnels for whatever reason.'

The sub-surface Stratford International station 'box' was complete – at 1,067 metres long, the same length as London's Tottenham Court Road. It is spanned by five bridges carrying roads and railway lines, and the station concourse, which was itself nearly complete.

In the north-east corner of the box, the single-line connection to the train maintenance depot at Temple Mills, just north of Stratford, was under construction. Transport Secretary Alistair Darling had confirmed in November 2004 that the new depot was to be built. Original plans had envisaged that Eurostars from St Pancras would gain access to North Pole depot in west London via the North London and West London lines, but it had been decided that recent increases in traffic on the already busy North London Line meant that Eurostars could not be accommodated without costly and disruptive infrastructure improvements.

Provision for the depot at Temple Mills was made in the CTRL Act, and the Government decision to bring construction forward was 'in the interests of

The Stratford station box in October 2004, looking eastwards; the existing 'National Rail' and London Underground station is in the top right-hand corner.
LCR/HAWK EDITIONS

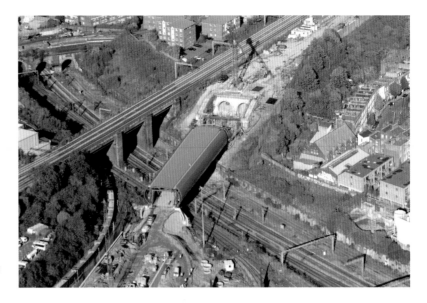

Work is in progress to cover the gap between the CTRL's bridge over the ECML and the London West Tunnel portal (temporarily stopped up), to honour an undertaking to keep the CTRL under cover all the way into the King's Cross Railway Lands. In the bottom left-hand corner a train is negotiating the link between the North London Line and the East Coast Main Line. LCR/HAWK EDITIONS

efficient operation of the CTRL service and the Eurostar fleet'. Access would be to European gauge, so it could be used by future generations of passenger rolling stock. The Government agreed in principle with London & Continental Railways to provide up to £402 million for the new depot package, which was not included in LCR's finance package for the CTRL. The depot would consist of an eight-road shed for Eurostar trains, with berthing sidings, train washers, and toilet discharge facilities. About £100 million of the cost was for land acquisition and compensation to tenants, and the total cost also included design and management costs, and allowance for contingencies (with work starting in winter, there was a significant risk of disruption of groundworks due to weather). The cost of the depot itself was about £250 million.

The financial package also included the transfer of Waterloo International and North Pole depot to Department for Transport ownership; in November 2004 Eurostar announced that it would switch its entire operation to St Pancras International station when the Channel Tunnel Rail Link was completed, rather than also keeping Waterloo International in operation, as had been envisaged.

TUNNELS AND TRACKLAYING

The completion of the London tunnels required three main concreting jobs. The invert or base of the tunnel was the first stage – sleepers would later be placed on it and concreted into place. The tunnels also have a continuous passenger evacuation walkway at door-step height, for use if passengers have to be evacuated from a train, as well as a lower-level examination walkway at the other side. With few straight or level sections, the tunnels' placement was designed in three dimensions, and the base slab pre-profiled for track cant (superelevation on curves).

The traditional, laborious method of constructing walkways would have been to lay and align the track, then set the walkway edge, with temporary shuttering to contain the concrete. However, by the time of construction, laser-guided surveying techniques meant that the walkway could be set in advance from the known design line of the rails.

All three main concreting jobs were carried out using slip form pavers, a novel

Major civil engineering work for the tunnels under London was completed in October 2004 – this is part of the St Pancras-Stratford section on the 20th of that month. LCR/QA PHOTOS

Tunnel Vision

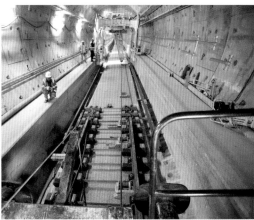

use of a machine familiar from its use in road surfacing. The laser-guided machines achieved 600 metres of concreting a day, working extended shifts.

Tracklaying on the Section Two route was in three distinct forms. On most surface track sections the same principle was adopted as on Section One: taking over the formation from the civils contractors as an 'unfinished road' – a very high-quality underlying formation – then assembling track on top, and lifting it through the ballast. This work was carried out in a slightly less mechanically intensive way than on Section One, said David Bennett, Implementation Director, Union Railways (interviewed for *Modern Railways* in April 2006) because of the relatively short distances involved.

The second form, laying track in concrete slab through the tunnels, was a very interesting engineering challenge, he said. High-speed railways in tunnels, and acoustic/vibration-isolated rails in tunnels, were relatively common, he said, but not the combination of the two, especially with high standards of attenuation set for the London tunnels. The solution used was a slightly softer and more highly engineered version of the TGV Méditerranée's Marseille tunnels. The design uses bi-block sleepers, with a rubber boot around each end, cast into the concrete, with an appropriately chosen pad under the rail, thus giving two levels of mitigation.

'The logistical support needed for tracklaying in tunnels is quite intense, but access for people is difficult,' continued David Bennett. Central to the method used was the 'concrete train' – a massive mobile concrete batching and placing plant – which, he said, 'was a huge success. The 450-metre-long train represented a big investment, but achieved very high production rates. As usual with bespoke plant, there were a tricky few weeks at the beginning of production when the target rates seemed ambitious, then a month later they seemed conservative.

'It's a very labour-intensive process but, with a fantastic team of workers, the limiting factor was the amount of concrete or rail that could be fed in. The basic principles are similar to ballasted track – build the track, set to final levels, but then concrete around the rubber-booted sleepers.'

'Setting out' was a key aspect, as on any high-speed railway, said David Bennett, but particularly so in the tunnels. 'Quite sophisticated methods were used – a continuous scanner referenced thousands of points per metre, and

Above, left:
Installation of the extruded concrete walkway in the Up-line tunnel east of Stratford on 19 May 2004, using a paving machine. LCR/QA PHOTOS

Above:
Thames Tunnel tracklaying: a multi-purpose gantry pulls long welded rail from a delivery train on 30 September 2004. LCR/QA PHOTOS

Part of the 450-metre-long concrete batching and placing train that helped achieve high production rates during tracklaying in the London tunnels. LCR/QA PHOTOS

Above:
Delivery of long welded rail for installation on rubber-booted sleepers in the London tunnels, April 2005.
LCR/QA Photos

Above, right:
Tracklaying in the London tunnels in April 2005.
LCR/QA Photos

Below:
The junctions and flyovers in the King's Cross Railway Lands in April 2007. Looking south towards St Pancras

(in the top right-hand corner of the photograph), from bottom to top the new routes are:

* *the new North London Line (NLL) to East Coast Main Line connection ('North London Incline')*
* *the CTRL to NLL connection for through running to the West Coast Main Line*
* *the main CTRL into St Pancras*

The Midland Main Line runs along the right-hand side of the photograph, and roughly parallel with it to the left is the viaduct for the St Pancras to NLL connection.
LCR/Urban Exposure

Left:
*Overhead catenary installation is under way on 26 May
2005 at Aveley Viaduct, where the CTRL crosses the
London, Tilbury & Southend line. The view is looking
westwards towards London.* LCR/Urban Exposure

virtually drew a digital rolled-out picture of the tunnel with the walkways, so you
could plot on that the kinematic envelope of your railway and the exact positions
for setting out the track, etc. There's perhaps nothing new in the technique, but
it was automated and probably done in a more sophisticated way than had been
done before.

'We were initially sceptical about whether some of it would give us the value
we needed, but it worked exceptionally well and the line and ride quality
achieved through the tunnels has been exceptionally good.'

*Overhead catenary works are in progress at Stratford
International, on the link to Temple Mills depot,
in February 2006.* LCR/Ros Orpin

Left:
*The overhead catenary system works near Ebbsfleet
in July 2005.* LCR/Urban Exposure

St Pancras International, viewed from the north in the autumn of 2005. Midland Mainline trains are using the interim station on the east side, where the three eastern platforms (11-13) will ultimately be used by CTRL domestic trains. Midland Mainline trains will move to the new western deck (platforms 1-4) in the summer of 2006. Six platforms extending into the Barlow trainshed will be for the 400-metre Eurostar trains. LCR/HAWK EDITIONS

The tunnels' ventilation fans were commissioned early, providing ventilation during the dusty work of fitting out. The equipment was then cleaned up for formal commissioning.

The third type of track runs from the London western tunnel portal across the King's Cross Railway Lands into St Pancras, where the railway standards are adopted from Network Rail – technically RT60 rather than UIC60 rail, with standard UK crossing forms.

A symbol of the completion of major railway infrastructure installation for the CTRL was a series of test runs by SNCF track and catenary measuring trains, after the first ever through trip in August 2005 from Paris to the King's Cross Railway Lands tunnel portal. Only minor adjustments resulted.

LAST STAGES

In April 2006, standing in the undercroft of St Pancras station, surrounded by the original cast-iron columns that support the train deck, it was possible to look up beyond the underside of the train deck to see the inside of the trainshed, where the former Midland Grand Hotel overlooks the station. One of three new apertures in the west side of the newly reinforced train deck made this view from undercroft into the trainshed possible for the first time.

The undercroft would house the main station facilities – passenger concourse, lounges and ticket halls – of the new St Pancras International station, with lifts and escalators carrying passengers to and from the Eurostar trains above.

The apertures in the train deck have been dubbed 'light wells', as they allow daylight into the undercroft, as well as providing access between train deck and undercroft.

'The status of the deck has been changed very substantially without fundamentally changing the form,' said David Bennett in the April 2006 interview for *Modern Railways*. 'There are some key ties that run across the shed from the arches – they used to take tension across the deck at the bottom of the arches, and we are transferring that through the structural integrity of the deck.'

As the new reinforced concrete train deck is supported on elastomeric bearings, expansion and contraction can take place at a different rate from the original structure below, relieving lateral pressure on the cast-iron columns that support the deck.

'Those massive light wells opened up on the west side will make the station work in its new form – the lifts and escalators are already in place,' said David Bennett. 'At the same time, we cut a great big slot – the Thameslink box – outside the trainshed, down on the west side, and also opened up the whole undercroft with its cast-iron columns to ambient air temperatures – it had all been enclosed before. Put it all together with modern loading standards, and you require a very

The first Eurostar has reached St Pancras during test running, on 6 March 2007. The light wells into the undercroft can be seen in the final stages of construction in this night view looking northwards within the Barlow shed. The effect of uplighting in the trainshed is clear. LCR/TROIKA

The first trains stand in the permanent Midland Main Line platforms on the west side of the St Pancras extension on 17 July 2006. LCR

A November 2006 view of work in progress in the St Pancras trainshed. Midland Mainline trains are using platforms 1-4 on the left (west) side of the station extension beyond the shed's north gable. LCR/Troika

Tunnel Vision

complex structural analysis of what you propose to do, and that was carried out by Arup.'

At the north end of the trainshed, an important discovery was the poor condition of the 'boots' that tied the northernmost arch to both the support piers and the wrought-iron tie rods that run through the platform-level deck. It had been planned to investigate the gable from a scaffold hung from this arch, to keep work going on at platform level (work had to run in parallel on roof, platform and undercroft levels, to keep to programme), but because of the arch's condition the scaffold had to be supported, which delayed work on that part of the deck.

'It then became absolutely fundamental that we got the gable work done as quickly as possible,' said Ailie MacAdam, Project Director of Rail Link Engineering, in an interview in October 2007. 'For one thing, when we opened the Midland Main Line station in July 2006, the public would be passing under the gable.'

Midland Main Line trains did successfully move to their new permanent location on the western deck extension on 17 July 2006, with passenger access through the St Pancras undercroft from the existing interim station entrance on the east side. The first public service to use the new platforms was the 06.10 train to Derby. It was an important event, because the Midland Main Line temporary track alignment cut across the Channel Tunnel Rail Link approaches, and moving it gave clear, unfettered access for the final works.

Work was also to start in summer 2006 on the £100 million hotel and apartment development at St Pancras, led by Manhattan Loft Corporation, with a new hotel structure on the west side. As the original hotel rooms in the famous Gilbert Scott-designed Midland Grand Hotel building at the south frontage of the station were not suited to modern needs, they were to become apartments or loft apartments, but the celebrated reception rooms would be restored. A 245-bed, five-star Marriott hotel was planned for the new western structure, with 69 apartments in the upper levels of the original building, which sold at between £0.5 million and £4.5 million.

'The choreography is very interesting,' remarked Dave Pointon, Managing Director of Union Railways, in an April 2006 interview for *Modern Railways*. 'We obviously have a lot of work to do to finish the construction project at St Pancras,

The interior of the Barlow trainshed, looking south on 11 January 2006 over one of the light wells opened up in the train deck, with the undercroft visible below.
LCR/CJW PHOTOGRAPHIC SERVICES

on the Barlow trainshed and the west section, then the fit-out operation on the station itself, then there is the hotel development. Add to that the Thameslink box fit-out, which we've just had awarded, and bringing alive the Midland Main Line station. You can also throw in the adjacent development work on King's Cross, including the Northern ticket hall, and the King's Cross Central development, which has just been given general planning consent by Camden Council.'

The view east from St Pancras's Barlow trainshed roof towards King's Cross station in February 2006, showing the blue-painted roof ribs before and after glazing, with the protective temporary screen below.
LCR/CJW PHOTOGRAPHIC SERVICES

The King's Cross Central site, which had also just received the endorsement of the Mayor of London, comprises 23 hectares (58 acres) of land lying between and behind St Pancras and King's Cross stations, available for development after the CTRL construction works. The majority of the site is controlled by LCR, and it and other parties were working with developers Argent on the development, planned to include 25 acres of new public routes and open spaces, and 750,000 square metres of mixed-use development, with 50 new buildings and up to 2,500 new homes.

'When finished,' Dave Pointon added, 'St Pancras station will be a fairly faithful reproduction of the original Barlow structure, probably seen as it's never been seen before, because it would have been polluted as fast as it was constructed in the 1860s.'

The new Temple Mills depot was about 70% complete by April 2006. An independent access railway line from Stratford was being provided, about 1.5km long; the depot's position close to the CTRL route is a huge advantage in terms of flexibility for Eurostar, said Dave Pointon.

Some rearrangement of CTRL stations will be needed for the 2012 Olympics, when CTRL domestic trains will form the 'Olympic Javelin' service running between St Pancras, Stratford and Ebbsfleet – but Dave Pointon commented that it would be a nonsense to interrupt the smooth conclusion of the CTRL project for preparatory works that were not yet fully defined. The main requirement would be alterations at Stratford, 'escalator capacity and so on to handle the large numbers of people expected'.

The interior of the Barlow trainshed at St Pancras in February 2006, looking north over one of the light wells opened up in the train deck, with the undercroft visible below. The first section of the new roof has had the scaffolding removed, allowing light to flood in at the far end. LCR/CJW PHOTOGRAPHIC SERVICES

St Pancras International is seen in this view looking north-east in July 2007, with the former Midland Grand Hotel at its frontage undergoing renovation. LCR/Troika

Stratford International, a view in February 2006 from the Up (London-bound) platform for domestic trains, looking east (away from London). The central platforms are for international services, with the connecting line to Temple Mills rising between them. LCR/Ros Orpin

Temple Mills depot, looking southwards (towards Stratford) in September 2005. The depot belonging to rail freight company EWS (which replaced one displaced from Stratford by CTRL construction) is in the foreground – it was later itself displaced by sidings for passenger trains, to replace a site to be used for the London 2012 Games.
LCR/Hawk Editions

A view from the west over Temple Mills Eurostar depot, substantially complete in April 2007. LCR/Urban Exposure

THE FINAL YEAR

On 14 November 2006 London & Continental Railways announced that Eurostar would start commercial services from St Pancras International exactly one year later, on 14 November 2007. On the same date, LCR made the announcement that the Channel Tunnel Rail Link project would now be known as 'High Speed 1'.

Rob Holden, Chief Executive of LCR, said, 'It is unprecedented that a major construction project of this size and scale is on track to be delivered on time and within budget.' The high-speed line would be completed with a total project cost of £5.8 billion, well within the overall budget for the project's funding established in 1998 of £6.15 billion, said LCR.

14 November 2006 also marked another milestone, when the last track panel was lowered into position on the Up Main Relief line to the north of St Pancras International. HS1 track was now in place all the way to the Channel Tunnel.

As part of testing and commissioning works, October 2006 had seen the final

Stratford International station, the hub for the London 2012 Olympics, looking east in the spring of 2007. The connecting line to Temple Mills depot can be seen rising on a flyover from the below-ground station box.
LCR/Urban Exposure

set of test-train runs on Section Two of the route. French Railways' Mauzin test coach, top-and-tailed by two Class 66 locomotives, used precision accelerometers to test track geometry such as line, level, gauge, cant and twist. In further tests, between 30 November and 7 December 2006, a Eurostar train was used over Section Two for the first time – though hauled by a Class 66 locomotive for tunnel ventilation system tests, including confirmation that

In late 2006 a Eurostar train was hauled by a diesel locomotive on CTRL Section Two for ventilation trials. This view shows locomotive No 66088 on the train on 4 December at Stratford, looking east. LCR/Eddie Macdonald

Tunnel Vision

predicted air flows could be maintained with a stationary train in the tunnels.

Energisation of overhead line electrification began in January 2007, and in March, after completion of static tests during the previous two months, Eurostar trains exceeded 250km/h (155mph) during dynamic testing on Section Two, after building up to 110% of the 230km/h (143mph) line speed. The first Eurostar train ran into St Pancras, platform 5, in the early hours of 6 March during tests. The first passengers to arrive at St Pancras on HS1 were International Olympic Committee officials, who travelled on a Eurostar from Stratford International to St Pancras International on 12 June, as part of an inspection of preparations for the 2012 Games.

LCR announced on 20 July that, following the handover of the final track and overhead line sections of HS1, Eurostar training and testing had begun, including driver training, route familiarisation and track testing, with two trains running from St Pancras to Ashford 12 times a day.

Above left and above:
Fitting-out and rail infrastructure installation are well under way in St Pancras in these February 2007 views.
Both LCR/EDDIE MACDONALD

A wraparound view of the west side of St Pancras in May 2007. A Midland Mainline inter-city train is visible through the transparent side of the station extension. LCR/SPHEROVIEW

A view south along the east side of St Pancras station's trainshed in July 2007. LCR/TROIKA

A Eurostar in St Pancras on a driver training run in July 2007. LCR/HUGO DIXON

Dappled sunlight bathes St Pancras station, shining through the refurbished trainshed roof as a Eurostar train visits the station on a training run on 4 October 2007. LCR/TROIKA

Eurostars on training runs stand inside the Barlow trainshed at St Pancras International in July 2007. LCR/TROIKA

Tunnel Vision

On 21 July the first Eurostar with passengers ran on (almost) the entire CTRL route. After stopping within the London tunnels, passengers took part in a trial evacuation onto a 'rescue' train in the adjacent tunnel, and in the Thames Tunnel a second evacuation trial was also carried out via a cross passage. The train returned non-stop from Westenhanger to St Pancras in about 29 minutes.

On 4 September 2007 Eurostar ran its inaugural train over Britain's new high-speed line. It achieved the fastest ever journey time between the French and British capitals, 2hr 3min. The train left Paris Gare du Nord at 10.44 local time, arriving in St Pancras International at 11.47 local time. It travelled at speeds of up to 320km/h (200mph) on the high-speed lines across northern France and in the UK.

On 20 September Eurostar ran the first train from Brussels into St Pancras International, taking 1hr 43min to cover the 373km (232-mile) distance, a new record for the journey between the Belgian and British capitals.

Temple Mills depot – officially dubbed 'Eurostar Engineering Centre Temple Mills' – was formally opened by Transport Minister Tom Harris on 2 October 2007. With eight 400-metre tracks inside the depot shed, Eurostar trains would no longer have to be split in half for maintenance or continually shunted around

St Pancras International, with a Eurostar on a training run, is seen from the north-west in July 2007. There are six central platforms for Eurostar, three eastern platforms (left of picture) for South Eastern high-speed services to Kent, and four western platforms (right of picture) for Midland Main Line services. LCR/TROIKA

A view south into the Barlow shed, with work nearly complete in September 2007. LCR/TROIKA

the depot, as at the former North Pole depot in west London, saving at least 2 hours per train visit. The depot is located 10 minutes' Eurostar running time from St Pancras International. A fail-safe protection system using swipe cards, the first of its kind, is provided to keep Eurostar staff safe while they work on the trains.

The depot is designed to house eight full trains, each 400 metres in length. The overall dimensions of the main shed are approximately 435 by 54 metres, with a floor-to-ceiling height of approximately 12 metres. Adjoining the main shed are a number of workshops, offices and the main administration building, together with a huge stores and materials shed.

Other features at Temple Mills include:

* an inter-road spacing of 6.5 metres, providing good working room for staff undertaking servicing/maintenance activities
* an automated overhead electrification system
* a bogie-drop design allowing two trains to be worked on simultaneously
* toilet discharge equipment for two trains to be cleaned simultaneously
* a bi-directional carriage wash, in which trains can be washed when moving in either direction
* automated wheel condition monitoring equipment
* nine overhead cranes, six in the servicing and maintenance building and three in the bogie-drop building
* 16km (approximately 10 miles) of track
* twice as much stores space as the previous depot, thanks to extensive 10-metre vertical racking.

Hitachi Rail Maintenance UK's depot at Ashford was opened by the Secretary of State for Transport, Ruth Kelly, on the same date, 2 October. Sited close to the CTRL, this was constructed for the Class 395 trains being built for high-speed domestic services between St Pancras and Kent via HS1.

The interior of 'Eurostar Engineering Centre Temple Mills' on the official opening day, 2 October 2007. BRIAN MORRISON

Eurostar half-set No 3308 in Temple Mills depot on 2 October 2007.
BRIAN MORRISON

Above:
Hitachi Europe officially opened its new train maintenance facility at Ashford on 2 October 2007 and displayed the first Class 395 train for Kent express services over the CTRL.
BRIAN MORRISON

Right:
A view of both floors of St Pancras at one of the west-side light wells. BRIAN MORRISON

A Eurostar and a new train for HS1 domestic services have arrived in St Pancras amid a spectacular light show during the Royal opening on 6 November 2007.
LCR/EDDIE MACDONALD

CELEBRATION

On 6 November 2007 HM The Queen, accompanied by The Duke of Edinburgh, launched High Speed 1, and officially opened St Pancras International station.

The Royal Party sat on specially built platforms beneath the Barlow trainshed roof and delivered an address to an invited audience of more than 1,000 guests, including senior political figures from London, the UK and Europe. A state-of-the-art light, sound and film show was accompanied by music from the Royal Philharmonic Concert Orchestra, performing with mezzo-soprano Katherine Jenkins and pop singer Lemar. William Henry Barlow was brought to life by actor Timothy West, telling the history of the station.

A pair of Eurostars and a Class 395 train for Kent high-speed services pulled in to the spectacularly illuminated trainshed within seconds of each other as part of the ceremony. The Class 395 train was diesel-hauled to the St Pancras approaches so that it could take part in the event, as it did not yet have approval to operate over HS1. It came in first, operating under an engineering possession, followed by the Eurostars.

The finale consisted of a film about the estimated £10.5 billion of regeneration attracted by High Speed 1, while the Queen met drivers from the Eurostar and Class 395 trains. Her Majesty was also introduced to those involved with the construction of the station, before unveiling an official plaque and receiving a posy of flowers and a specially made clock featuring a dial in the style of the St Pancras trainshed clock.

Rob Holden, Chief Executive of London & Continental Railways, said: 'The completion of High Speed 1 and the opening of St Pancras International, on time and within budget, is a great source of pride for the thousands of men and women who have been involved in one of the most significant projects in UK railway history. For Her Majesty to have been here to officially declare the new high-speed line and station open is a fitting tribute.'

On 14 November 2007 Eurostar launched services from St Pancras International, following a 15-hour overnight move from Waterloo International. The first departure, bound for Paris, left at 11.01, saluted by the Royal Philharmonic Concert Orchestra.

In a ceremony before departure, Eurostar UK Chief Executive Richard Brown and Friends of the Earth Executive Director Tony Juniper named the train *Tread Lightly* – the title of Eurostar's initiative to reduce its environmental impact.

Celebrations, entitled 'Waterloo Sunset' in honour of the song by the Kinks, marked the closure of Waterloo International on 13 November. They included live music, and local dance and theatre groups performing on the departures concourse. Eurostar had launched international rail services from Waterloo International on 14 November 1994 and had carried more than 81 million passengers.

Journey times between London and the continent were cut by about 20 minutes from 14 November, with non-stop times between London and Paris of 2hr 15min, London to Brussels in 1hr 51min, and London to Lille in 1hr 20min. Infrastructure improvements in Brussels meant that an improvement of about 24 minutes for services to the Belgian capital had been achieved, compared with 2006 journey times. Trains were scheduled to reach the Channel Tunnel portal from London (111.6km) in just under 31 minutes.

Eurostar began services from Ebbsfleet International station on 19 November. The first departure was the 05.38 for Paris. Dame Kelly Holmes, winner of two Olympic gold medals, officially opened Ebbsfleet International on 29 January 2008. Eurostar journey times from Ebbsfleet are 10 minutes less than from St Pancras International.

Close to Junction 2 of the M25 motorway, Eurostar boasted that Ebbsfleet

Above:
Sculptor Paul Day's 'The Meeting Place' – made in bronze, more than 9 metres high and weighing more than 4 tonnes – overlooks St Pancras International. The statue was commissioned by London & Continental Railways. LCR/MICHAEL WALTER/TROIKA

Below:
The statue of the poet Sir John Betjeman, by sculptor Martin Jennings, was commissioned by London & Continental Railways, cast in bronze and installed in St Pancras in October 2007. Betjeman and the Victorian Society were among the campaigners against the mooted demolition of St Pancras in the 1960s. LCR/TROIKA

Above:

Roland Hoggard, seen at his home in Thurgarton, Nottinghamshire, recovered and restored the original Dent clock, which was damaged when being removed from St Pancras station in the 1970s. LCR/MICHAEL WALTER/TROIKA

Above right:

The new Dent clock is installed at St Pancras in October 2007. Dent & Co was commissioned by LCR *to provide an exact likeness of the original, damaged in the 1970s. Dent took castings of remnants of the original decorative chapter ring, hand-restored the castings, then hand-poured new mouldings in aluminium. These were fixed to the dial,* also made in aluminium, welded and polished. The hour and minute markers were cut from English slate, and English gold leaf was used to finish the numerals, hands and banding. The clock is controlled by GPS signal. LCR/TROIKA

Below, left:

Departing passengers take the moving walkway from the departure lounge to their Eurostar train on the first day of services from St Pancras, 14 November 2007. LCR/TROIKA

Below, right:

The departure lounge in the St Pancras undercroft on the first day of use, 14 November 2007. Travellers wait alongside exposed original brickwork. LCR/TROIKA

Passengers leave (and some stop to photograph) a Eurostar train that has arrived in platform 10 at St Pancras on the first day of services there, 14 November 2007. LCR/TROIKA

A view across to the west side of the St Pancras trainshed on its first day of Eurostar services, 14 November 2007. LCR/TROIKA

Ebbsfleet International station in April 2007, looking from the south along the CTRL towards the Thames Tunnel. The connecting route to the North Kent line is the railway line (with its platforms) diverging to the right.
LCR/URBAN EXPOSURE

Ebbsfleet International station in April 2007, looking south with the connecting lines to the North Kent line on the left.
LCR/TROIKA

Below:
The St Pancras Champagne Bar ready for customers in November 2007. LCR/EDDIE MACDONALD

station had 2,500 parking spaces within 5 minutes' walk of the check-in gates, and that the charge of £11.50 a day was significantly cheaper than London's main airports. A total of 9,000 car parking spaces is expected to be provided by the time of the 2012 London Olympic and Paralympic Games. Domestic train services using the CTRL were planned to begin in late 2009, providing connections at Ebbsfleet from many parts of Kent; meanwhile a bus service linked the station with Dartford, Greenhithe, Gravesend and Swanscombe stations.

St Pancras Thameslink station opened on Sunday, 9 December 2007, replacing King's Cross Thameslink station. The Transport Secretary, Ruth Kelly, officially opened the station the next day. Passenger access is from the north end of St Pancras International, with seven escalators and two lifts providing access to the platforms.

The main missing piece in the operational railway jigsaw in St Pancras itself was then the South Eastern domestic express services to and from Kent using HS1, due to start in late 2009. An important part of the supporting infrastructure – London Underground's Northern ticket hall, to the east of the

Ebbsfleet International station in April 2007. LCR/TROIKA

Below:

No 319428 leads the 09.25 Bedford-Brighton service into St Pancras Thameslink station on 10 December 2007, the date of its official opening. BRIAN MORRISON

station – remained under construction, as did several retail areas within St Pancras itself, and the redeveloped former Midland Grand Hotel. Stratford International station was expected to open in 2009 for Kent express services, with Eurostar services still to be decided on.

Open and doing a roaring trade on day one, 14 November 2007, was St Pancras's much-publicised Champagne Bar – at more than 90 metres, the longest in Europe, said LCR – which runs next to platform 5 and the light wells linking the station's train-deck level with the undercroft. It was therefore a high-profile pathfinder for the concept of St Pancras as an attraction in its own right – with a variety of shops and restaurants modelled on Grand Central station in New York.

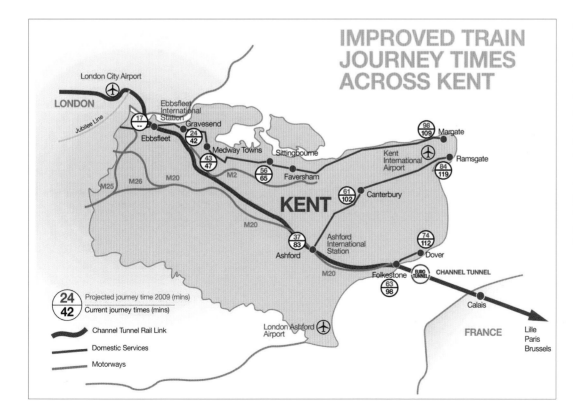

IMPROVED TRAIN JOURNEY TIMES ACROSS KENT

A map of express services between Kent and St Pancras, planned to start in December 2009, using the junctions between the CTRL and existing lines at Ebbsfleet and Ashford. Folkestone and Dover trains will leave/join the CTRL at Ashford. The 'current' journey times were 'average', not the fastest possible in 2007 when this map was issued. SOUTH EASTERN TRAIN OPERATING COMPANY

5 Facts and figures

IN-CAB SIGNALS

THE CHANNEL TUNNEL RAIL LINK adopted the TVM430 cab signalling system, as used on France's TGV-Nord and Belgium's high-speed lines. The CSEE Transport (later Ansaldo) TVM430 was one of the systems originally installed on the Eurostar train, avoiding alterations to an already complex train.

Signal interlocking is also carried out by the TVM430 system, the version of TVM introduced on the TGV Méditerranée line in France shortly before Section One of the CTRL opened. Other TVM applications used relay technology, but the new interlockings were integrated into the processors that run TVM, using solid-state interlocking-type technology.

In the cab, the driver has a numeric indication of the maximum speed and advance information about when that speed is going to change. A steady display means that the speed shown applies at least to the end of the next block section, while a flashing display (still showing the current authorised speed) indicates a need to slow down by the end of the next block section. The system is permissive – the driver may pass a marker at which the train has been stopped, provided it is not protecting a junction. After doing so, three red squares are displayed, indicating that the driver should proceed on sight, supervised by the ATP to a maximum of 30km/h (18mph).

Block sections are about 1.5km (0.9 mile) long on flat track, and a minimum of four block sections to stop from 300km/h (186mph) gives a comfortable braking curve 'without spilling the coffee'. There are no lineside signals, just the blue sign with yellow chevron that marks the end of each block section, and the point at which the train should be brought to a stand if necessary. A further block section beyond the 'target stop' marker to the 'protection' marker (the last behind a preceding train or obstruction) gives in effect a 1.5km overlap.

The length of block sections varies on hills: careful modelling set out to achieve the shortest possible lengths, with a variety of train speed characteristics to be catered for, to give as much capacity as possible without compromising safety or functionality.

The system includes automatic train protection (ATP), which supervises driver performance to ensure adherence to the speed limits: there is a small degree of tolerance above indicated speed, but no warning if the driver is getting close to the limit. The only intervention is an emergency brake application, a regime believed to encourage defensive driving.

Opposite:
Part of the proposed King's Cross Central redevelopment.
ARGENT/GMJ

A Eurostar running from London passes signalling section indicator boards as it leaves the Singlewell freight loops behind, 6km (3.5 miles) from the Medway, on 15 October 2003. LCR/QA Photos

Trainborne equipment communicates through data frequencies superimposed on track circuits; these are electrical currents carried in the rails, which are picked up by coils on the train. (The basic principle may be familiar from the Victoria Line on the London Underground.) TVM430 uses 31 different frequencies, any one of which can be present or not. The frequencies represent characteristics such as gradient, target speed and block length, which the on-board computer uses in calculating what to tell the driver and ATP system. Different speed bands are selected by TVM's network code for the TGV-Nord high-speed line in France, Eurotunnel and the Channel Tunnel Rail Link. The trackside equipment can feed track circuits up to 7km (4.3 miles) away. The CTRL route is signalled for reversible running.

RLE and Union Railways investigated other signalling systems, but one factor in the choice of TVM was that it gave a consistent medium for the drivers on the CTRL, through the Channel Tunnel, and onto TGV-Nord.

TVM430 extends to the western portal of the London tunnel. As the speed bands in the TVM system are not applicable to platform approaches, there is lineside signalling in the St Pancras area, along with the trackside-beacon-based KVB train protection system, already fitted to Eurostar trains and used in France between Gonesse and Paris Nord. (KVB stands for 'contrôle de vitesse par balises' – speed supervision by beacons.)

At Ashford, trains taking the route through the international station switch to UK-pattern lineside signalling. When running on lines without cab signalling, the TVM cab display is blank, with the driver taking authority to proceed from lineside signalling.

GSM-R RADIO

The European railway cellular-radio system, GSM-R, is installed on the CTRL. Section One was its first application in the UK, but initially only for lineside mobile communications.

GSM-R is designed to provide secure communication between trains and control systems. 'There were early but unrealised expectations in some quarters that it would be ready for CTRL Section One,' said David Bennett, Union Railways' Implementation Director in an April 2006 interview. 'There was a stronger belief that it would be available for Section Two, but it hasn't been. So Section Two is replicating the Section One approach, with analogue Cab Secure Radio as our main driver-to-control radio system – this means we have twice over placed "the last order ever" for this system!'

GSM-R was in place as background infrastructure, and used for operational and maintenance purposes, with provision for migration to GSM-R cab secure radio.

FREIGHT

Express, lightweight freight could of course be carried in Eurostar-type trains over the CTRL, but use of the route by more standard freight trains required careful consideration of design standards. Adaptation of the line for freight trains was promoted by rail freight industry representatives, though the argument that the CTRL's main benefit for freight would be to free capacity on other lines was advanced by the line's developers.

Passing loops for freight trains were provided on the CTRL in accordance with assurances given to Parliamentary Select Committees during consideration of the bill that authorised the new railway.

A connection between the CTRL and the existing rail network is provided at Ripple Lane, Dagenham, and there is also a direct connection between the CTRL and Dollands Moor freight marshalling yard near the Channel Tunnel. Freight could also use the junction between the CTRL and North London Line near St Pancras.

The Lenham passing loops are seen on 24 February 2002 in this view looking towards London, with infrastructure installation continuing. LCR

As a result of aiming to limit environmental impact, the CTRL curves and climbs to follow the landscape and existing transport corridors: there are only two main stretches where the railway is horizontal, totalling 4.5km (2.8 miles). Less than a third is straight, while 10.5km (6.5 miles) is on gradients of between 2.4 and 2.5% (1 in 40). The main locations of gradients at or near these figures are:

* approaching St Pancras (climbing west towards the tunnel portal)
* on both sides of the Thames Tunnel
* climbing east from Ebbsfleet
* climbing on both sides of the Medway
* climbing east from the Boxley valley
* climbing west from Ashford
* climbing from the Channel Tunnel.

Interviewed in October 2001, Union Railways (North) Managing Director Chris Jago said that making provision for freight trains with a maximum speed of 140km/h (87mph), which may only achieve 80km/h (50mph) on steep gradients, had been the problem of devising a cant (superelevation of track on curves) that satisfied both high-speed trains and lower-speed, heavier-axleweight freight. As well as the track wear from heavier axle loads, slower-moving freight trains could also cause heavy rail wear (and experience heavy wheel wear) on curves superelevated for high-speed trains. Superelevation of rails on the CTRL's curves is between 160 and 180mm, compared with about 210mm on most high-speed routes in France.

CTRL maximum axle loads for international and domestic passenger trains are set at 17 tonnes, and 22.5 tonnes for freight or (theoretical) locomotive-hauled passenger trains. Due to the maximum gradient, trains composed of vehicles fitted with standard UIC 85-tonne couplings are limited to a maximum trailing load of 1,100 tonnes. The maximum train length for freight is set at 775 metres.

A presentation to freight operating companies by Network Rail (CTRL) in advance of the opening of HS1 indicated that charges might work out at more than double the rate per mile for other Network Rail routes. Maintenance costs (and therefore charges) would be higher than for other lines because of the high track quality standards required for high-speed trains.

For daytime operations, capacity for freight trains was expected to be available (at off-peak times), but the current performance regime would compensate Eurostar at £700 to £1,000 a minute for any delays caused to its services, and it was thought unlikely that freight operators would want to bear this risk.

For night-time freight services, lower penalties would apply and capacity was expected to be available five nights a week – three nights per week with single-line working for CTRL maintenance, with two spare nights reserved for ad hoc infrastructure work or testing. On Saturday and Sunday nights the route was expected to be closed for maintenance.

POWER

The CTRL has a 25-0-25kV overhead catenary system – feeding at 50kV enables greater distance to be maintained between feeder stations while maintaining the voltage profile under heavy current demand (up to 550 amps for a Eurostar). The power supply is connected across the feeder wire at minus 25kV and catenary at plus 25kV, earthing via the rails.

The overhead line electrification follows French practice, with 'universal column' masts, an aerial earth wire, feeder wire, and conductor and catenary wires (5.08-metre contact-wire height) supported on a cantilever arm, and a buried earth cable connected to the masts at intervals. The equipment is sectioned at intervals, depending on the position of switches and crossings. Neutral sections use an isolated section of contact wire about 200m long.

Pantograph settings on the two Eurostar power cars have to be adjusted before they enter and after they leave the Channel Tunnel, in which the power supply contact line is 5.92 metres above rail level to accommodate the tall Eurotunnel shuttle trains. For the changeover, pantographs are lowered while the trains coast through a neutral section separating the two systems, and are raised to the adjusted position when the rear power car is also in the new section; this entails some loss of momentum. To minimise this, the CTRL/Eurotunnel voltage changeover is located near the CTRL 100km marker, 9km (5.5 miles) from the Channel Tunnel. Approaching the tunnel, the changeover is made during the reduction from the CTRL 300km/h to the Eurotunnel 160km/h line speed; coming out of the tunnel the gradient is such that the changeover could not be made in the Dollands Moor area.

The wire height through Ashford International station platforms is set at a minimum of 4.68m.

LOADING GAUGE

The CTRL is built to UIC 'C' gauge, except through Ashford International station, where the biggest passenger gauge, B+, applies. The typical formation width is 14,000mm, with tracks at 4,500mm centres.

The CTRL's new stations have UIC-height platforms for international trains and Network Rail-height platforms for domestic trains.

SAFETY

The CTRL set a goal of zero accidents, and the Target Zero Truck – an initiative suggested by site workers themselves – toured construction sites to deliver the message that individuals were responsible for their own safety.

A Health and Safety Breakthrough Programme focused on safety leadership training; eliminating unsafe behaviour; daily pre-task planning; near-miss reporting; and nine key safety issues. Individual contracts were rewarded for reaching 250,000, 500,000 and 1,000,000 man-hours worked without a serious accident, with sums of money donated to contractors' nominated charities.

A number of serious accidents did, however, occur during CTRL construction:

* a worker was fatally injured near Westenhanger in March 2003 in an incident related to overhead electrification
* in May 2003 a scaffolding worker died after a fall in a plant room at the northern portal of the Thames Tunnel
* two men died as a result of a fire in August 2005 on a construction train travelling through the CTRL's Thames Tunnel

* a miner was severely injured in the North Downs Tunnel in 1999 when a large
lump of rock fell from the tunnelling face.

ENVIRONMENT

To limit environmental impacts, about 85% of the CTRL route is in tunnel or within existing transport corridors (next to existing motorways, major roads or railways).

On Section One, 12 million cubic metres of spoil was moved and recycled on site, much of it used for false embankments ('bunds').

The CTRL project planted 255 hectares of mixed broad-leaved woodland, of which about 30 hectares is on translocated ancient woodland soils; 40km of new hedgerows; 200 hectares of grassland, including 46 hectares of wildflower grassland; 3 hectares of reedbeds, alder carr and wet grassland, and 1km of ditch.

Twenty kilometres of specially developed noise barriers were built where there was no room for earth bunds – the barriers are typically 4 metres from the track and 2.5 to 4 metres high. They are made of timber, are 350mm thick, and are machined and bonded to absorb sound, with absorbent material added in sensitive areas. Low-level 1.4-metre steel barriers were designed for bridges, placed inside the parapets close to the noise source and lined with absorbent material.

More than 100 hazel dormice were translocated to new breeding grounds in central England as part of an English Nature repopulation scheme. Thousands

*An illustrative plan of King's Cross Central,
the redevelopment scheme centred on the railway lands
north of St Pancras station, which is at the south side,
centre left.* Argent/Townshend Landscape Architects/Quickbird

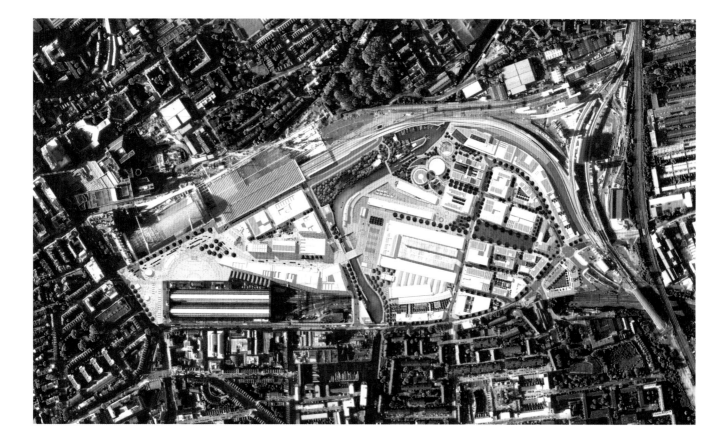

Tunnel Vision

of bats, badgers, amphibians, reptiles and water voles were moved away from the CTRL route to new habitats, including artificial badger setts and bat nesting boxes.

An impression of Granary Square, part of the proposed King's Cross Central redevelopment. ARGENT/GMJ

ARCHAEOLOGY

The CTRL team reckoned that the archaeological investigation process related to the new railway was the biggest of its kind undertaken in Britain. Finds along the route included an Anglo-Saxon burial ground at Cuxton, near the Medway, while at Thurnham, north of Maidstone, detailed excavations of a Roman villa took place.

At Saltwood in east Kent an Anglo-Saxon grave was discovered to contain artefacts of national importance, including a gold and silver brooch studded with garnets and emeralds.

REGENERATION

A figure of £10.5 billion has been placed on the value of economic regeneration levered in by High Speed 1.

The adoption of an easterly approach route for the railway was intended to help regenerate the area known as the Thames Gateway, in east London, Thurrock and north Kent. When London & Continental Railways won the concession for the high-speed line in 1996, it established its Stations & Property division to acquire the land on which the railway would be built, manage adjacent property, help regenerate the area through which the railway runs, and set up its stations that would act as catalysts for regeneration.

An impression of Coal Drops Yard, home to shops, galleries and restaurants – part of the proposed King's Cross Central redevelopment. ARGENT/GMJ

This applies at the King's Cross Railway Lands adjacent to St Pancras, the Stratford Railway Lands, which will now be central to the main 2012 Olympic and Paralympic Games, and the former cement workings close to the north Kent station at Ebbsfleet. At King's Cross and Stratford, where LCR owns the lands, a 50:50 profit-share arrangement with the Government applies, while at Ebbsfleet, where cement group Lafarge owns much of the land, planning permission for development stimulated a profit clawback to the Government. The King's Cross lands are being developed by London & Continental in alliance with Argent. The mixed-use development at Stratford is being adapted to suit the 2012 Games.

	Section One	Section Two	Total
Length of double track (km)*	74	39	113
Tunnel length (km)			
Excavated	3.2	22	25.2
Cut and cover	3.2	1.04	4.24
Structural open cuttings (km)	1.7	1.76	3.46
Excavated material (million cubic metres)	12	2	14
Number of bridges			
Rail (under)	41	19	60
Road (over)	53	9	62
Foot	23	7	30
Viaducts (km)	2.7	1.62	4.32
Retaining walls (km)	7.0	-	7.0
Track ballast (tonnes)	-	-	850,000
Number of sleepers			
Ballasted track	248,000	67,000	315,000
Slab track	-	69,000	69,000
Electrical feeder stations	2	1	3
Auto transformers	13	5	18

* Section One includes 5km Waterloo connection, Southfleet Junction-Fawkham Junction

Normal minimum curve radius (metres)

Section One   4,000

Section Two   2,400 (250m minimum outside St Pancras)

CTRL capacity

Maximum 8 International plus 12 Domestic train paths per hour (one direction); 5 International plus 12 Domestic per hour at St Pancras (as estimated by Union Railways in the 1990s)

Out-turn construction and land purchase costs

Section One   £1.9 billion

Section Two   £3.9 billion

(Department for Transport figures; excludes Temple Mills depot)